Irresistible

FOCUS YOUR ENERGY • EXPERIENCE TRUE LOVE

TRINA PETERSEN

T0163681

NASHVILLE

LONDON • NEW YORK • MELBOURNE • VANCOUVER

Irresistible

FOCUS YOUR ENERGY • EXPERIENCE TRUE LOVE

Published in New York, New York, by Morgan James Publishing in partnership with Difference Press. Morgan James is a trademark of Morgan James, LLC. www.MorganJamesPublishing.com

The Morgan James Speakers Group can bring authors to your live event. For more information or to book an event visit The Morgan James Speakers Group at www.TheMorganJamesSpeakersGroup.com.

ISBN 9781683508137 paperback
ISBN 9781683508144 eBook
Library of Congress Control Number: 2017916177

Cover Design by:
Rachel Lopez
www.r2cdesign.com

Interior Design by:
Christopher Kirk
www.GFSstudio.com

In an effort to support local communities, raise awareness and funds, Morgan James Publishing donates a percentage of all book sales for the life of each book to Habitat for Humanity Peninsula and Greater Williamsburg.

Get involved today! Visit
www.MorganJamesBuilds.com

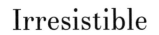

Irresistible

Advance Praise

"Pastor Trina Petersen's book *Irresistible* lives up to its title. Her creative writing style, faith-filled wisdom, and her FOCUSed commitment to care for women flows from every page. The candid illustration of her pastoral/coaching interaction with women at the start of each chapter anchors her advice in the day-to-day struggles of real people. The wisdom imparted by Pastor Petersen in her "acrostic" format provides powerful insights into becoming irresistible in your relationships through the irresistible love of God. Turing these insights into action will produce life-giving transformation, renewal, and restoration in the individual reader and in their relationships.

"This book was designed for women but the process for personal transformation is equally true for men. This is an excellent resource for couples to study together. It is faith-based and biblically centered. Her personal transparency is both helpful and refreshing. Her mature understanding of love and relationships that reflect the nature of Christian community focused on responsible behavior, accountability partners, and the benefit of coaches who have experience in working through complex relationship affirms the truth that you do not have to be alone in the midst of such tragic circumstances. Her advice and direction is consistent with the path of discipleship.

"*Irresistible* is an excellent resource for encouragement and guidance for those who long for irresistible love, who long to become irresistible people, and who long to love others with that same irresistible love. Don't miss the opportunity to fully utilize the wisdom contained in this book. It truly is irresistible!"

~ **Rev. John Bradosky**, Bishop of The North American Lutheran Church

"Pastor Trina Petersen's book, *Irresistible,* is indeed irresistible! The introduction alone is enough to stir the hearts, emotions, and sensibilities of most women I know from a diversity of races, nationalities, socio-economic, educational, and spiritual backgrounds. It's a woman thing! We've all experienced some part of what Trina shares so eloquently in her tough but loving manner. What most of us have not experienced, or experienced much later than we would have preferred, is the magnitude of wisdom she imparts. Wisdom that cuts deep into the soul and pares away the mess and confusion... wisdom that makes you want to be real with yourself... wisdom that shows you how to move from realization, to action, to healing, to joy, to content-ment, and to PEACE! Get and give this diamond of an irresist-ible book, sisters! "

~ **Pat Funderburk Ware**, President & CEO of The Ware Development Group

"I am in total awe thinking about the lives this book is going change. *Irresistible* is quite inspirational and very empowering. It will help you go where you never thought possible because you were not thinking I'm possible, and had forgotten that everything is possible with God. Let the lessons begin as the conversations start. Thank you, Author/Coach Trina, for an awesome and motivating read!"

~ **Latina Bryan**, Founder and CEO of Chapter 42

"Rev. Petersen has a winsome and economical way with words that makes concepts and spiritual truths easily accessible for everyone. In *Irresistible*, she drills down using imaginative acronyms to unveil and impart biblical truths that will yield hope and healing in both women and men. This is a 'must read' for everyone seeking healing and wholeness for the broken places in life."

~ **Victor J. Belton**, Campus Pastor, Concordia College New York
Vice President of Leadership, Director of The Center for Contextual Leadership

"If you're still dazed and confused concerning your love life after reading this book, it's nobody's fault but your own. The information in this book is both practical and universal. I appreciate Trina's transparency in sharing her own life experiences as well as the memorable acronyms she included to help guide us to 'irresistibility.' This isn't just another self-help book. It's a self-hope and a self-love book sent directly from God through Trina to help his children — definitely a must-read!"

~ **Alacia LaRobin**, Recording Artist

"Trina Petersen is a bonified prolific writer, innovative thinker, and gifted coach. One whose amazing experiences and gifts have awarded those in her path the sheer essence of a coaching experience that the produces healthy relationships. *Irresistible* is a combination of her unique skill to help people understand the realities of true, lasting love through Scriptures. *Irresistible* is incredible and irresistible."

~ **Victoria L. Burson**, Sr. Pastor and Certified Professional Coach

Dedication

Anndrina and Kajarra, you inspire me to keep
moving forward, to be all I was created to be and to
leave a legacy. I thank God for the gift of you.

Oh, that you will forever be amazed by God's grace,
smitten by His love, and moved by His Spirit!
Irresistible life is yours to have and keep!

*For You formed my innermost parts; You knit me
[together] in my mother's womb.*
*I will give thanks and praise to You, for I am fearfully
and wonderfully made; Wonderful are Your works,
And my soul knows it very well.*

Psalm 139:13-14(AMP)

Table of Contents

Introduction

"Love is patient, love is kind. It does not envy, it does not boast, it is not proud. It does not dishonor others, it is not self-seeking, it is not easily angered, it keeps no record of wrongs. Love does not delight in evil but rejoices with the truth. It always protects, always trusts, always hopes, always perseveres."
~ *1 Corinthians 13:4-7 (NIV)*

Toxic Love, Tainted Sources

Love is supposed to be patient, kind, and caring. At least, that's what the Bible says. And you believe what is written. So how come your relationship experiences are complicated and full of drama? Is love supposed to cause so much pain? Is love supposed to be so confusing?

You are not asking for anything out of the ordinary. Nor are you expecting flawless perfection. You just want to love and be loved. You have sought the advice of your friends and family. You have read books and Googled all types of articles on true love, where to find a good man, and how to catch him and keep him. You have followed "the 12 steps for making a man respect you" and "the 5 steps on how to create a happy relationship" and still, you find yourself frustrated, aggravated, and angry.

Maybe love really is a game, a game you don't know how to play well. Or maybe it's not the game at all. Maybe it's who you are playing the game of love with. After all, you know what you want — peace, happiness, and true love. But for some reason, the men you enter into relationships with just don't seem to get it. How hard can it be to find one man who is single, psychologically mature, emotionally available, financially secure, and spiritually grounded?

It seems like every relationship you enter is one where you are expected to give, give, and give some more. You go above and beyond giving what is needed and what is wanted, but no one is giving you what you need. How are you supposed to hold it together when life is pulling you apart? Are you tired of smiling on the outside while you are crying on the inside? Are you tired of receiving toxic love from tainted sources?

Desperation

Jasmine was desperate. "If I don't find a man soon ..." was her opening statement to a list of misfortunes. If she didn't find a man soon, she would become an old maid, she would be too old to have children, and all of her best years would be behind her. If she didn't find Mr. Right, she would not be able to pursue her dreams of going back to school, starting a business, and traveling around the world. Jasmine was certain that not being in a supportive, loving, passionate, and committed relationship was causing her dreams and her life to fall apart.

When I asked Jasmine, what was stopping her from getting that man, her answer surprised me. "I think my problem is where I'm looking," she said. "I'm looking in the wrong places, that's why I'm finding the wrong men. I need to focus on finding the right place to find the right man. And when I find him, I need to be ready."

"Ready?" I asked.

"Yep, ready," she replied. "I don't want to have to chase him. I want him to chase me. I want to be irresistible so that he will chase me. I want to be wined and dined and swept off my feet, just like in the movies. I don't want to have to worry about money, because he'll have enough. That way I can focus on building a business. We can get married and have a family and travel around the world."

Jasmine had a clear picture of what she wanted and how he would provide what she wanted. He was going to text and call her several times during the day, prepare romantic dinners for her, and make passionate love to her. Jasmine knew without a doubt that being single was robbing her of her happiness, peace, and future. She was ready for things to change, and she knew that being in a loving relationship was all the motivation she needed to get her happy and her sexy back and make her dreams become reality.

Real Talk

I agreed with Jasmine: Her situation was costing her. However, from my perspective, "he" was not the cause of Jasmine's unhappiness. Her perspective was the cause of her distress, and from that perspective, her woes originated with "him." It didn't matter who the man of the hour was, and it didn't matter if she was in a relationship with him or not in a relationship with him. It was always about him, and blaming him was a convenient and comfortable way for Jasmine to avoid dealing with the real issues.

Jasmine's desperation was causing her to make rash decisions that were impacting her financially, physically, emotionally, and spiritually. She applied for loans and borrowed money to buy him stuff. She invited and moved him into her home. She found herself at the clinic because of an STD she caught from him because she made the decision to sleep with him. She found herself isolating from friends and family because she made the decision to withdraw from them. Yes, her desperation was causing her dream to be deferred and yes, her heart was becoming sick, but she was the one making the decision to pursue him and postpone her dreams. Jasmine's decisions were driving her circumstances. Changing the way she made decisions would change the life she was living.

From my perspective, as her life coach, Jasmine was living the life she helped to form and shape. This being the case, she had the power to reform and reshape it. Although she could not see it, I could clearly see that her life was the cumulative outcome of her decisions. Her ability to change her focus would enable her to regain her power, a power she had given away. Jasmine needed to find when and where she had lost her power so she could reclaim it. She needed to identify when and where she had lost her peace, her happy, and her sexy so she could go back and regain them. Jasmine needed to find out when and where she had lost herself and her future, so she could go back and reframe them.

Jasmine was right in that she was looking in the wrong places, and that was the reason she was finding the wrong men. Jasmine and I would spend the next several months searching the right places, so that she would become the irresistible lady she wanted to be and experience the true love she wanted to experience.

Facing Fear

Jasmine was ready for change, yet she feared the process and the unknowns of changing. Reclaiming, regaining, reframing, and renaming sounded good, but it also sounded like more than she could do. The thought of failure overwhelmed her. What if she failed? How would she rebound? Failed relationships and lost love had already drained her. Her finances, emotions, and body were, in her words, a mess. Where would she even start? How do you begin to fix something that's so messed up? Just thinking about it was causing Jasmine to panic. "Breathe, Jasmine," were the words I spoke. I assured her that if she was willing, she was able. She didn't need to overwhelm herself with the process of changing. If she would commit to focusing on specifics, change would occur. And the framework on how to focus was one I could provide for her.

The Shift

My hope is that your experience of love is not like Jasmine's, that your decisions are not causing you to surrender your power to experience love into the hands of a "him." My hope is that you shift your focus, and instead of focusing on him, you focus on finding and defining your voice, power, and authority to transform your life. But my hope for you is not what matters. What matters is *your* hope for you and what *you* are willing to do to get what you are hoping for. Your issue may not be toxic love and unsatisfying relationships. Perhaps you are experiencing other unsatisfying areas in your life. Either way, my questions to you remain the same, "If I provide a framework that changes the way you experience love and helps you cultivate peace and pursue your dreams, will you shift your focus? Are you willing to change how you make decisions and approach relationships? Are you open to dismantling counterproductive behaviors that cause you to resist what you want and open your mind and heart so you become irresistible?" If your answers are yes, then this book was written just for you. It will show you how to start and supply you with what you need for the journey.

CHAPTER 1

From Pieces to Peace

*Living in pieces focuses on the losses
of the past. Living in peace focuses
on the gift of the present. The move
from pieces to peace is a matter of
transforming the mind.*

More Than a Notion

"Why do all the crazy men find me?" Jasmine was sitting in an oversized chair in my office. This was my first time meeting with her as a client, though it was not my first time hearing the complaint. It is a sentiment many of the women I coach express. Jasmine just didn't waste any time getting to the crux of the issue: "If I could just find a good man who was committed to loving me, we could take on the world."

Jasmine was young, attractive, and educated. She was quick to let me know that she had a good job and a nice car, and attended church almost every Sunday. But despite all she had accomplished and acquired, Jasmine was still unhappy. Before Jasmine arrived at my office, she had already concluded where the source of her woes could be found. She was convinced that her unhappiness, lack of interest in life, and recent weight gain were all because she could not find "a good man."

Jasmine was convinced that there were few good men left, and she was determined to find one. So she dated as often as possible. Virtual dating, speed dating, blind dating — Jasmine was on a mission to find a good man, one who supported her dreams and encouraged her to move forward. And though the dating scene was what she called "brutal," she was determined. There was no doubt in Jasmine's mind that the right man would give her the energy and confidence she needed to move forward, and she was certain that having that man would help relieve her of some of her financial burdens. Not only would she have someone to help her to pay for the things she enjoyed having, she would also have someone to help pay for the things she liked doing and have some-one to do them with. Jasmine was sure that the absence of a man in her life was the source of her problems.

She was also sure that not having a man was causing her unhap-piness. How could she be happy when she was alone? "Most of my friends are booed up," she said. "I come home to an empty house."

Broken Pieces

When Marie walked into a room, it appeared that she had it all together, that her life was on lockdown, and that she was in control. She had purchased her first house at the age of 21 and had it paid off by the time she was 30. She had her own business with multiple clients. She drove a nice car and had money in the bank. If material possessions were the indicator, Marie was doing better than good. Unfortunately, how things looked was not how things were. Appearances can be deceiving.

While everything looked good externally, Marie was experiencing internal chaos. By the time she was in her thirties, she'd been married and divorced several times. Her first marriage took place when she was 21 years old. He was gainfully employed, disciplined, and intelligent. She felt they had much in common, and so she married him. What Marie didn't know was that he would abuse her mentally, emotionally, and physically. When that relationship ended in divorce, she vowed that she would never do "that" again. "That" was to date or marry anyone who had similar characteristics to her ex-husband.

Marie's next serious relationship was with a young man whose personality was what she considered totally opposite from her first husband's. They dated for about a year before they married. That marriage lasted a bit longer than the first, but he was emotionally unavailable. Eventually his irresponsibility and infidelity were too much for Marie to handle, plus the void she was trying to fill remained empty. She was not alone, but she was definitely lonely.

> *"A thief is only there to steal and kill and destroy. I came so they can have real and eternal life, more and better life than they ever dreamed of."*
>
> John 10:10 (MSG)

Broken

Failure began to gang up on her and flood her psyche. Marie couldn't understand why she kept attracting men who were emotionally unavailable, men who would not commit. At times, her sense of emptiness was so intense that Marie sought to fill it even when she knew the relationship held no promise of a future. She just wanted to love and be loved. Surely that was not too much to ask, was it?

In time, Marie's experiences began to define her character. Her feelings of unworthiness caused her to enter into relationships where she was mistreated. Her esteem was in a downward spiral. Her life was becoming a contradiction. But she needed to hold it together for the public eye. So that's what she did. Marie put on a good show. She cried at night, but she laughed among family and friends. She was an internal wreck, but she performed with excellence at work. The same mouth that sang praises at church complained and devalued men. Her bitterness was becoming visible through her words and actions. She felt she needed to keep it together, and that she couldn't let anyone know how or what she was feeling. All she needed to do, she thought, was focus and bring the fragmented pieces of her life together so she could have some peace in her life. So, she directed her energy into presenting the appearance of having it together, a role she played well. Marie actually thought she was okay. But she wasn't.

She was so focused on external appearances that she denied that internally, she was crumbling like coal in the fist of a strong hand. She was so stressed out that she would pull the car into her driveway and get out without putting the car into "park." She would leave water running and walk away, causing sinks to overflow. She would leave her house keys hanging in the outside door lock overnight and lock her keys in the car. She was losing control. But she didn't reach out for help. She thought she could handle it.

The Awakening

Marie thought she was in control, but she was living a life of insanity. She thought each relationship was new and different, but in truth, though the men were different, many of their characteristics were the same. It was like she was choosing the same "gift" wrapped in different wrapping paper.

One day, in desperation, Marie had a conversation with God. "What am I doing wrong?" she asked. "How can I be so successful in business and a failure at love?" God very clearly impressed in her spirit that there was a common denominator in the successes and failures of her life. She had been a part of every experience.

The revelation caused Marie to change her prayer. She stopped asking God to fix the men. Marie invited God into her broken, messed-up life and asked Him to fix *her*.

When Marie asked God to step in and fix her, she was thinking He would do a quick fix. What's that saying? If you want to make God laugh, tell Him your plans. Needless to say, God had a different plan. Getting her life together was a process, a process that included dedication, discipline, and — hardest of all — cooperation. Even though Marie was the one who wanted change, even though she was the one who agreed to do it God's way (her way had not worked very well), she found that all too often she was not working with God, she was working against Him.

Marie's desire for success in love was strong, but her ability to experience love was tainted by her past experiences. Her desire to trust was tainted with suspicion. She was plagued with negative thoughts that whispered that her history made her unlovable. Why would anyone want to love her? Marie struggled with the process, but she stuck with it. She faced numerous obstacles and challenges, but she was determined to find and enjoy pure, lasting love.

Marie learned that the biggest obstacle in her path to enjoying love was not external, it was internal. She learned that she was going to have to stop sabotaging herself, stop operating from pride, and stop trying to please everyone if she was going to move forward. She was going to have to deal with the issues that had caused her to lose herself, and for that, she would need help.

Her business savvy and intellect were not going to change her love life. She wasn't going to be able to reason her way through it or BS her way around it. As much as she did not want to admit it, how to find and enjoy true love and a lasting relationship was beyond her. She really needed help, help that she didn't want to ask for.

The Encounter

Marie's help came as soon as she was able to admit that she was not in control. This positioned her for what she calls, "The Encounter." The Encounter was a divine revelation that the unhealed hurts, unmet needs, and unresolved issues of her childhood were impacting her ability to give and receive love. Marie knew enough to know she didn't know enough, so she read, participated in groups and activities that gave her sound biblical teaching, and found someone she could trust to talk to. She needed a safe place to release some of the secrets she had been holding. (Actually, she found out that she hadn't been holding the secrets, the secrets had been holding her — in bondage!) Her life began to transform.

Finding Peace

Marie credits accountability for having a major role in her transformation. Accountability to God, herself, her coach, and accountability partners. Without accountability, Marie is not sure how long it would have taken to gain the courage, strength, and tenacity to focus and stick with the process of getting her life together. Even now, fear attempts to hinder her, but accountability keeps her focused and moving forward.

I know firsthand the challenges and setbacks Marie struggled with while on her journey from a life burdened by the weight of a heart and soul broken into pieces, to a life filled with peace. I know how much courage it took for her to overcome her feelings of unworthiness and begin living an irresistible life. I know because I am Marie.

From Pieces to Peacemaker

I know what it's like trying to hold it together while in the whirlwind and chaos of life. I know what it's like to be angry at yourself for caring so much, for desiring him so much, for giving so much of yourself without getting the same in return. I know what it's like to have a void in your heart that desires to be filled so badly that you settle for counterfeit love just so you can be held and hear those three desired words. I've been where you are, and I know how to get unstuck.

My journey to wholeness has taken many years, lots of trial and error, and an ocean of tears. I kept telling myself that if I could withstand the trials and pressures of life, that one day I would emerge as a diamond. I finally came to the realization that I could spend as much time under as much pressure as I could stand, but the coal in my life was not going to turn into diamonds. I was going to have to realign my thought process and choose to live differently if I wanted a life that had the brilliance and value of a diamond. So, I reached out for the help. I sought the help of psychologists, counselors, coaches, accountability partners, and friends. Some of the counsel and advice I received was helpful. Some was not. Some was wise, godly counsel, some was theory, and some was opinion. But I kept walking and moving forward, trusting that God would complete the work He began in me.

Walking through the process has equipped me with experience and wisdom. I am familiar with the challenges, pitfalls, and road-blocks of the journey. And the fact that I know how to navigate through them will save you precious time.

I cannot live in freedom knowing that my sisters are in bond-age. My heart becomes heavy when I encounter women who are living in chaos, brokenness, and loneliness. Escaping from the pit of tainted love and living in the freedom of irresistible love has blessed me with the gifts of love, peace, and joy. These gifts were not given to me to hoard. They were given to me to share with others. One of my favorite quotes was spoken by Harriet Tubman. She said, *"I freed a thousand slaves. I could have freed a thousand more if only they knew they were slaves."* Like abolitionist Tubman, I am passionate about helping the enslaved realize their freedom has been taken away by tainted, toxic love, and walking with them on the path that leads them to the freedom of irresistible love. I rejoice every time another sister is set free! I am filled with unspeakable joy when she walks in the power and authority given to her and experiences true love.

Hannah's Story

When I met Hannah, she was timid and withdrawn. She questioned and was apologetic about nearly everything she said and did. Her self-esteem was extremely fragile. According to Hannah, her plight began at birth. She was the third of four children, and the only girl. Growing up had been especially hard for her. Her brothers treated her like one of the boys and criticized her if she acted "too much like a girl." No matter how hard she tried to please her father, he always found a way to criticize and belittle her. Hannah had determined early in life that being "invisible" was her best weapon of defense. Over the years, she'd perfected it. The problem was that invisibility was not producing the outcome Hannah wanted.

Hannah wanted to be happy, to have peace, and to marry and have a family. She wanted her opinion to be valued, her actions to be appreciated, and to be respected. Hannah wanted love — to love and be loved. Her typical demeanor of being withdrawn did not attract the kind of men that appealed to her, and her sporadic outburst of anger did not help her maintain the relationships she did manage to establish.

When Hannah accepted my invitation to journey with her, she was hopeful that things would change. What Hannah didn't realize is that *she* would change. Transformation began to occur internally. That transformation enabled her to work on her relationship with her father and reconcile with him before he transitioned to the afterlife. Transformation has caused her relationship with her brothers to improve dramatically. It has given her courage to use her voice, raise her expectations, and pursue her dreams. She has not gotten married yet, but she has found peace; she found and maintains her happy, and she is enjoying irresistible love.

The FOCUS Framework

The secret to change is to focus all your energy, not on fighting the old, but on building the new. ~ Socrates

FOCUS Fix

If it's not broken, don't fix it. It's a popular saying in our culture, and implies, I would guess, that things that *are* broken should be fixed. Finding a fix in this day and age is simple for most things. A quick search-and-surf on the computer yields a multitude of suggestions on how to "do it yourself."

You know exactly what I'm talking about. How many searches have you done in an attempt to fix your love life? Your searches revealed both quick fixes and complicated fixes for finding and keeping a man, some of which you even implemented in your life. Yet, you still are not experiencing the love you want. Well, I have good news for you. You can stop fighting the old and begin building the new by changing your focus. That's right! FOCUSing is the solution to experiencing the love you want. The journey is laid out for you in this book, so you don't have to figure how or where to begin. You have already taken the first step in making the decision to read this book. Your next step is making a commitment to FOCUS not on finding a man, but on building the new. "The new what?" you ask. The new, irresistible you.

Your desire is to become irresistible and to experience true love. The way you experience your desire is to open yourself to irresistible love. You receive what you are open to, whether it's a thought, a feeling, or an experience. And over time, your experiences, both positive and negative, shape your thoughts, beliefs, attitudes, and behaviors. This includes the conscious and the unconscious, the real and the perceived, the distractions and the intentional, the dilemmas and the successes, the drama and the triumphs of life. They all have influenced and impacted your life in ways you may not be aware of. Ultimately, they are the reason you are living the life you are living. When it comes to relationships, it doesn't matter if you have experienced multiple failed relationships or no serious romantic relationships; there is one common denominator in all your experiences. The FOCUS framework helps you to put your energy into building up the common denominator so that irresistible love is the new experience. Oh, and by the way, the common denominator I am speaking of is you.

You are the one person who has been in all your relationships. Therefore, it is safe to surmise that you — your thoughts, beliefs, attitudes, and behaviors — are having an impact, both positive and negative, on your relationship outcome. It's like the coal and diamonds I mentioned earlier. Both begin as carbon compounds. However, molecular alignment determines if the outcome is coal or diamond. By putting your energy into FOCUS, you will gain wisdom and develop the skills you need to realign your thoughts, beliefs, attitudes, and behaviors. And just like with diamonds, you will learn how to make informed choices by learning about the 4 Cs of love: Clarity, Color, Cut, and Choice. Being equipped will help you distinguish true love from toxic, make informed decisions, and begin to experience happiness, peace, and the long-lasting relationship of true love and passion you desire.

FOCUS Design

This book is designed as a guide to ensure that you are not overly focusing on or ignoring the negative events of your history. And even though you may want to avoid or forget some of your history and focus only on your best life experiences, the truth of the matter is that, placed in the care of God, all of your experiences work together for the good. Notice that I said "work together for the good." In no way am I suggesting that all your experiences have been good. I am saying that having a FOCUSed mindset can help you examine and reframe every experience so that the good can be discovered and utilized.

FOCUSing will empower you to take off the designer mask you have been wearing. I call it designer because you have put a lot of time and energy into developing and designing a mask of who you want others to think you are while you hide who you really are and how you honestly feel. When you FOCUS, you are able to look in the mirror, take off the mask, and deal with the reflection of the first person you see. You gain the power to deal with your hurt instead of denying it. You begin to deal with the unresolved issues instead of dismissing them. You gain the power to address your unmet needs instead of diminishing them. The FOCUS framework is designed to help you honor your experiences in totality and frame them in a way that enables you to open your heart, soul, and spirit to the irresistible love you want.

The FOCUS Framework

The FOCUS Framework provides you with five keys to unlock the doors of your heart, soul, and spirit. It is probable that these doors are currently closed, separating you from peace, happiness, and irresistible love. Entrusting you with these keys gives you potential power and authority to open yourself to receiving the love you want. To help you overcome the whelm and overwhelm of the process, each key of the FOCUS Framework is structured in the form of an acronym. This will hopefully help you remember the components of each key. The five keys of FOCUS are:

F — Figure It Out

O — Optimizing Through Observation

C — Changing Point

U — Utilizing to the Max

S — Securing Irresistible Love

The five keys to FOCUS are like any other keys. They hold the potential to unlock locks, but they are only useful if you use them. It doesn't matter if you are dealing with a padlock, a door lock, or a combination lock, you have to know how to use and work with the key. This book provides you with the keys of FOCUSing, but you are going to have to work the keys to unlock the doors that stand between you and irresistible love.

Each key of FOCUS lays out the objective, provides instruction, and offers a plan of action to help you pull it all together. This is not just a good book to read, it is a guide for transformation. Be prepared to engage emotionally, psychologically, and verbally. The temptation to resist sharing that you are on a transformational journey is going to be real. But even more real is your need for guidance and accountability. Be prepared to inform and invite someone you trust to journey with you. This will provide you the guidance, support, and accountability you need to stick with the process and experience the irresistible. Commit yourself to a life of FOCUS.

The last, but most important aspect of this book is the origin of the writing. This book emerges from, is grounded in, and is filled with the love, grace, and mercy of God, the accuracy of His Word, and the power of the Holy Spirit. There is no way for me to talk about love and not talk about God. God is love. Learning of and embracing God's love, positions you for a life in which nothing is missing or wanting. Love never fails. Learning and embracing God's grace will cover you during the journey and carry you when you cannot move forward. God's grace is sufficient. Learning and embracing God's power will strengthen and liberate you. God's power is made perfect in your weakness. Resist God's love, grace, power, and word, and you resist limitless possibilities. Embrace God's love, grace, power, and word, and experience the power of the irresistible.

Handing Over the Keys

Having the five keys gives you potential power and authority. Knowing how the keys work empowers you to use the keys appropriately, saving you from the frustration of trying to unlock a combination lock with the use of a card key. I am handing you the keys in this brief summary, so you can begin to focus and gain clarity on how you will use each key.

F — Figuring It Out

Before you fix anything, you have to figure out what the problem is and the desired outcome. The three chapters in this section are dedicated to helping you figure out your beliefs, desires, and obstacles. Figuring out these three aspects of your life will give you clarity of vision and prevent you from fumbling and stumbling in darkness.

✓ *Figure out your BELIEFs.* Because your beliefs directly impact your thoughts and behaviors, the first thing you will need to do is to figure out what you believe and how that belief was formed.

✓ *Figure out your DESIREs.* Your desires work with your beliefs. They impact your thought process, emotions, and behaviors. Figuring out your desires will help you identify and eliminate undesirable patterns of thoughts, emotions, and behaviors.

✓ *Figure out your OBSTACLEs.* What specifically is preventing you from experiencing your desired outcome? Naming the obstacle is important, because once you name it, you can call it out into the open. And calling it out causes it to lose its power.

O — Optimizing Through Observation

When fighting a battle, strategy and coaching are critical to victory. Coaching provides non-judgmental objective insight. Strategy allows you to optimize your resources. This requires observation. Careful observation allows you to gather information. Gathering information informs the application, and the application produces transformation. Having these notches on your key will help you unlock barriers that have been preventing you from moving forward.

- ✓ **OBSERVE** the origins of your thoughts, attitudes, and behaviors. This allows you to evaluate how you are approaching love. Having an awareness of how you are operating will inform you of the areas in your life where change needs to occur.

- ✓ **OPENness** of heart, soul, and spirit are essentials in your ability to experience irresistible love. It helps you establish healthy motivations for change and postures and prepares you for transformation.

- ✓ **OBEY** helps you with timing and expectations, both of which are critical to transformation. If your timing is not in sync with God's timing, a good thing during the wrong season can be a burden. If your expectations are not in alignment with God's promises, you are setting yourself up for disappointment.

C — Changing Point

You have now gained enough intel to provide you with the information necessary for change. As you engage in the exercise provided in this key, you will begin to experience change. The changes you make will promote transformation in your life.

✓ **CONFRONTing** your reality takes courage and skill. You are stronger than you think you are and you have skills that you may not even be aware of. Honing in on your courage and skills will enable you to confront the obstacles that have been preventing you from experiencing your desires.

✓ **COMMENCE** and let change begin! Working the framework presented in this chapter guarantees change in your life! Now, I don't want you to get anything twisted. Work the framework and change will occur. However, the output of the process is determined by your input. So give it your all, and embrace the revealing of the new you.

✓ **CONQUER** what you confront. Your reality may cause you to think differently, but you were born victorious. Use the knowledge you are acquiring and defeat the aspects of life that have been defeating you. Learn to live in the truth that victory really does belong to you.

U — Utilizing to the Max

Experiencing irresistible love is not an experience of luck or happenstance. It is the product of intentional and strategic action. The objective is for you to experience irresistible. The strategy in this key is for you not to think thoughts of defeat, but to utilize what you already have.

✓ **UNDERSTAND** what you have. Lamenting about what you don't have will not move you toward what you want. In fact, most often you will find that when you complain, you remain. Understand, be grateful, and give praise for what you do have, because you have what you need.

✓ **USE** what you have. Now that you understand what you have, it's time for you to use what you have. You don't have to wait for someone or something to change. Change is subject to you. Your current situation is the perfect space and opportunity for you to use what you have so change can occur.

S — Securing Irresistible Love

Positioning and posturing yourself to receive irresistible love is probably some of the most intense and intentional work you will do in your life, and once you experience it, you want to ensure that you keep your focus forward. There is a way to make sure that you remain open to receiving irresistible love: It's a matter of you standing firm and staying respectful of the love you are receiving.

- ✓ **STANDing** firm is a daily choice and discipline. It requires that you exercise and balance trust and action. It's a matter of you understanding that when you have done what you need to, stop engaging in busy work. Stand still and let God be God.

- ✓ **STAYing** respectful is also matter of choice. When you choose to respect, you choose to maintain the posture that keeps you open to receiving the love you want. When you choose to respect God and yourself, the experience of love cannot resist you, nor will you resist the love.

Bringing Your Love into FOCUS

Your love life is out of focus, and you say you're ready to fix it; you are ready for change. Using the FOCUS framework will bring you the outcome you desire. It will work, if you work it. It will produce your desired result, if you trust and follow the process. What you don't want is to do is to talk about change, go through the motions of change, resist change, and stay the same. With that being said, before you move forward, make the decision that you are ready to change and make a commitment to yourself that you will change. Focus all your energy on changing. Change how you think about love and prepare yourself to approach love differently. When you bring your love to FOCUS, you are bound to see love more clearly and experience true love on a deeper level. So, get ready to figure out, observe, change, understand, and stand exactly where you want to be, in the midst of irresistible love.

CHAPTER 3

Figure Out What You Believe

The love may be pure, but if the belief system is faulty the experience is one of faulty love. Know what you believe so your beliefs don't taint your experience of love.

Your beliefs are impacting the way you think, feel, and behave. They are impacting your attitude about and perception of experiences and events. What you believe to be true becomes your truth. Therefore, it is important that you gain clarity on what you believe, what you desire, and what is blocking you. If your love life is not what you want it to be, check and change what you believe. Otherwise, you will always attract the same experience.

Candice

Candice and Johnny met at church several years ago. At the time he was handsome, kind, and active in the young adults' ministry. Since he had many young ladies to choose from, Candice was excited that Johnny had chosen her. They dated off and on for years. The early days of their relationship were filled with laughter and good times. They did everything together. They went grocery shopping together. They ran errands together. Johnny chose a hair stylist for Candice and paid for her to get her hair done weekly. Johnny even took and picked Candice up from work. Candice believed she was lucky to have a man who gave her so much attention. After a year of dating, Johnny proposed to Candice. She accepted. "Who wouldn't want to marry someone as wonderful as Johnny?" she said. However, Johnny's moods began to intensify, and the changes were not so wonderful.

One day, Candice went shopping with her co-workers during her lunch break. That evening, when Johnny picked her up from work, he inquired about the shopping bag. When Candice shared news of her lunchtime shopping spree, Johnny told her how disappointed he was with her choice to shop without him and informed her that she was to eat lunch during her break, not go shopping with the girls. From that day forward, Johnny periodically popped in for surprise lunch dates.

Candice sat before me because she needed help. She shared the dynamics of her relationship with Johnny, concluding with the statement, "I feel so bad. He is such a good person. He takes such good care of me. He does everything for me. More than my daddy ever did for my mother or me. I don't understand why I feel like I'm trapped."

Candace was operating on a faulty belief system which translated Johnny's actions of controlling into actions of love. Candice believed that Johnny did what he did not because he was controlling her, but because of his love for her. She believed that the more he controlled her, the more he was declaring his love for her. Candice's journey to irresistible love required that she examine and change her belief system.

> *Immediately the father of the boy cried out [with a desperate, piercing cry], saying, "I do believe; help [me overcome] my unbelief."*
>
> Mark 9: 24 (AMP)

Laying It Out

Your beliefs directly impact your thought process and your actions. Consider Candice. Her belief was that the more a man loves you, the more he does for you. Unfortunately, because her experience as a child was one where attention and affection from her father were lacking, Candice developed a faulty system of beliefs and values that left her unable to distinguish between attentiveness, affection, and control. If you believe you are unlovable, you will develop and live by the core belief that nobody loves you. This core belief will impact your ability to give and receive love.

One of the challenges of living today's fast-paced life is maintaining the ability to have beliefs rooted in pure love. God is pure love, and His love for you is undeniable. This truth is in competition with the realities portrayed in Hollywood, as well as a host of other influences that are informing your belief system. Until you are intentional about knowing what you believe and hold as important, you will continue to fumble through relationships and life. The acronym BELIEFS will give you clarity on why it is important for you to know what your beliefs are, so you can know where you need help for your unbeliefs.

BELIEFS

B — Building Blocks

Your beliefs are building blocks for your life. They are foundational in shaping your thoughts, and your thoughts impact your behavior. You could say that the life you are living is based on your beliefs. If this is the case, and you are not living the life you want to live, then one of the first things I encourage you to do is to look at your belief system. What convictions do you hold to be true? When it comes to love and relationships, what do you believe love looks like or feels like? Scripture says you are to love God, yourself, and then others. What are you using to build your relationships, and what order are you building the relationships in?

E — Expectations

Your beliefs inform and shape your expectations. If you believe you are lovable, you expect to be loved. If you believe you are unlovable, you expect and accept less than loving treatment. I once heard a gentleman tell a young woman, "If your man treats you like a doormat, and you let him treat you like a doormat, then you must think you're a doormat." Your expectations are an outlook framed by your beliefs. You will accept what you expect. One way to decipher what you believe is to evaluate your expectations.

L — Launching Pad

Your beliefs are a platform for launching love. They provide a supportive mental and spiritual framework that gives you the energy you need for lift-off. When your beliefs are skewed or unstable, your behavior and outcomes may be volatile, distorted, or aborted.

I — Intimacy

Intimacy within a relationship is more than sex. It is the closeness that develops through sharing. Being open to sharing spatially, psychologically, physically, emotionally, and spiritually is how you experience intimacy. And because you are a spiritual being having a physical experience, spiritual intimacy is the most powerful of them all. I have learned that the only way to experience *intimacy* is to be open to allowing someone to *into-me-see*. Openness comes with vulnerability. And the idea of vulnerability may scare the bejeezus out of you, but stay with me.

What do you believe when it comes to intimacy? What has your experience been? Are you ready to share the good, the bad, the beautiful, and the ugly on a spatial, psychological, physical, emotional, and spiritual level? Figuring out your beliefs and openness to intimacy will help you understand why you've been experiencing the degree of intimacy you have.

E — Empowerment

Knowing what you believe provides you with the power to overcome your fears. Right now, your fear is using false evidence in an attempt to make a negative outcome appear real. It is tapping into your negative emotions of past experiences to inform your contemporary and future experiences. However, having beliefs that are founded in the truth reveals the lies and sets you free from the false evidence, giving you the power to move forward in the truth. Faulty beliefs and weak core values lend themselves to faulty and weak relationships. Beliefs based in truth result in true love and strong, lasting relationships.

F — Feed Your Thought

The relationship between beliefs and thoughts is intrinsic. The thoughts running through your mind at any given time are many. But those thoughts don't have any power or become reality until you believe them. Beliefs are thoughts to which you give power. The thoughts you feed are the thoughts that gain power. What are you feeding your thoughts? Where are you getting the food from? If your thoughts are being fed from tainted and toxic sources, then your beliefs are going to be tainted and toxic. Feeding your thoughts from a source of purity, the Word of God, will nourish your beliefs with power to produce.

S — Set Your Course

The life you are living is a reflection of your beliefs. Your beliefs have been working with your thoughts to shape your attitude, behaviors, and character. Because you want to experience love that is irresistible, your beliefs, attitudes, and actions need to be in alignment with love that is irresistible. Another way for me to say this is to say that you cannot say you want irresistible love and then resist that love. Set your beliefs in alignment with the irresistible love of God and allow your beliefs to set your course.

Bringing Your Beliefs into FOCUS

Your beliefs are like a GPS (God's Protective System) in life and love. They navigate you to your desired destination. When you drift off course, they get you back on track. They tell you when you need to exit, make a U-turn, or when you have arrived. Unfortunately, if failed relationships are part of your history, either you are not honoring your beliefs, or your beliefs and desires are not in accord. You may be choosing to take your own path, a path that may be scenic, but is taking you to the wrong destination.

Living out your beliefs takes intentionality, strength, and courage. It requires you to do some internal searching as opposed to external seeking. It will cause you to walk away from someone negative even if he is talk, dark, and handsome. It will require you to steer clear of someone who may be good to you, but is not good for you. The more you live your beliefs, the more rewarding and pleasant you and your life will be.

Your beliefs are shaped by what you hear, see, and experience. Your experiences help you to develop an opinion that you hold as true and immoveable for that time. Changing your love life will require you to take time and evaluate if you are basing your beliefs on something solid, immoveable, and true, or if your beliefs are based on something unreliable, changing, and faulty. You want to be happy, have peace, and experience true love, and you want it now. But before you jump out of the frying pan, take the time to figure out what you believe. This way, you will have clarity on what you believe, what your core values are, and why you do what you do. Answer the following questions so you can begin to figure out your beliefs:

1) What are your building blocks to serve as the foundation to your relationships?

_____

_____

_____

_____

2) What are the characteristics of God's irresistible love?

_____

_____

_____

_____

3) What do you expect to give in your relationships?

_____

_____

_____

_____

4) What do you expect to receive in your relationships?

_____

_____

_____

_____

5) What inspires you? What characteristics attract you to love?

_____

_____

_____

_____

6) How open are you to irresistible love? How do you resist love?

_____

_____

_____

_____

7) Are your current beliefs about life empowering you or sabotaging you?

_____

_____

_____

_____

8) What source(s) are you using to feed your love? How regular and how balanced a diet are you feeding your love with?

_____

_____

_____

_____

9) Moving forward, how will you allow you beliefs to set your course?

_____

_____

_____

_____

CHAPTER 4

Figure Out What You Really Want

You will never begin to live the life
you desire to live until your desire to
change outweighs the fear of change.
Allow God to give you your desires and
transform your life.

Changing Desires

All Amy ever wanted was the American dream. She wanted to grow up, get married, have a house and children, and live happily ever after. She wanted to get manicures and pedicures and massages. She wanted to go on weekend getaways and summer vacations. She wanted her husband to pay the bills and take care of the car. How she ended up being the breadwinner for the household, the primary caregiver for the children, the manager of the finances, the mechanic, and the planner of every outing was beyond her. How her life had ended up in such a mess was beyond her comprehension. Her husband was able. He was an executive team leader. He knew how to get people on the same page to work together. How had their relationship gotten so off track? She had prayed, asking for a man who could provide her the lifestyle that she wanted. She thought Derrick was the answer to her prayers. He was a good provider, but he was never at home. Amy was at her wit's end. Something, either Derrick or her desires, needed to change.

> *Delight yourself in the Lord, and He will give you the*
> *desires and petitions of your heart.*
>
> Psalm 37: 4 (AMP)

DESIRES

Your desires are a sense of longing or hoping for a person, object, or outcome. Because you have a desire for love, you have already determined the who, what, and how of your love manifestation. You have already pictured in your mind what he will look like, act like, and how he will make you feel. Your desires emerge from your beliefs. So once you have clarity from Chapter 3, you can begin to build upon that foundation to determine what you want. The acronym DESIRES provides a framework that attracts irresistible love.

D — Divine

Knowing what you desire is critical when it comes to entering into a relationship. Relationships framed by superficial desires, material things, physical appearance, etc., usually end up being unfulfilling in the long run. In turn, the quest for deep, meaningful, fulfilling, and long-lasting love is a desire that comes from God. God is love, and God wants you to experience love. That is **why** you have the desire to love and be loved. This is not the Hollywood kind of love with scripts, directors, lights, camera, and action. The desire you have for love is a divine desire. So, if you are looking for love in the wrong places, from the wrong faces, during the wrong time and spaces, you are setting yourself up for a wounded heart and unmet needs.

God's love is pure and true. Making the decision to receive His love is a decision to receive unflawed love. His love is perfect and it comes with no strings attached. When you open up before God and make the decision to hold nothing back from Him, God will do what needs to be done.

E — Emotionally Driven or Discerning

One of the hardest things you will do is to wait for the deepest desires and longings of your heart to be fulfilled. God, the Giver of Dreams and the One who placed the desires deep inside of your heart, has a plan that includes timing and maturity. He has given you gifts, skills, and talents. Your ability to distinguish between an emotionally driven relationship and a God-ordained relationship will save you a lot of heartache. Discernment is your ability to put your emotions to the side long enough to hear from God and know God's will. One of the last things you want to do is to get ahead of God.

S — Season

Knowing what you want is one thing. Receiving what you want is another. Receiving has a lot to do with knowing what season it is. Just because you want something right now doesn't mean that now is the best time for you to have it. You may have dreamed of marrying the cute, popular football player in high school, but at *16,* you were not ready. And, yes, I know you are not *16* anymore, but the reality is that timing is everything. You may bake wonderful cakes, but a half-baked cake is in no way appetizing. There is a time and a season for everything. Understand what season this is. This is your season to prepare for love by focusing on yourself. It is time for you to get to know yourself, take care of yourself, and love yourself. Trust God on the timing. After all, your desire for love comes from God, and He will fulfill those desires when you are ready.

I — Investigate Your Involvement

You will delay experiencing your desired relationship if you engage in the practice of finger-pointing and fault-finding. It was easy for one of my clients, Amy, to put the burden of their relationship issues on Derrick, on what he was doing and what he failed to do. What Amy did not realize was that the life she was living was a result of her decisions. Please do not misunderstand me. In no way is Derrick perfect. Nor does Amy have any control over Derrick's actions. What Amy does have a say in is her behavior. Just like Amy, you can move forward in love as soon as you stop looking at the speck that's in his eye and begin to deal with the log that's in your eye. I know these words seem harsh, but trust me, they are spoken in the spirit of love.

You cannot continue to blame the man for your failed relationship without investigating your involvement in the brokenness of the relationship. This will keep you from operating in insanity. You know, doing the same thing over and over and expecting different results. Two halves may make a whole when you're talking about oranges, but two broken people participating in a relationship does not make a whole or healthy relationship.

R — Reacting or Responding

Your last relationship was impacted by your behavior of reacting and responding. If you are more likely to react, your relationship was probably more volatile, laced with arguments, door slamming, and the like. Reacting is emotion-driven and defensive in nature. It happens when you are uncomfortable with something that is being said or done. Reacting can cause emotions to show up without any reasonable driving force. When you react, you are no longer in control. In fact, you have given control to the one who is saying or doing whatever is making you uncomfortable. If you are a reactive person, you may be thinking that you react because you are such a passionate person. You know I don't want you to get things twisted, so let me set things straight. You can be passionate, but your passion needs to be centered, on purpose, and controlled. Not unexpected, unproductive, and out of control.

The flip side of the coin is responding. There is still some external stimulus that causes you to respond. However, responding is more thoughtful and contains reasoning. Responding is guided by emotion and undergirded by faith. Responding looks forward to an expected end. Consider responding in the context of your relationship. Responding can change the direction of an interaction. You can even respond with passion. Responding is a sign of growth and maturity. It requires you to engage, grow, and have awareness of your emotions, triggers, and thoughts. The main difference between responding and reacting is mindfulness.

E — Examination

When your desires are in divine alignment, you begin to experience life in a positive and new light. Bringing your desire into alignment will most likely require you to ask God to examine your desires. This is not the kind of examination that you pass or fail. It is the kind of examination where you invite God in to examine your heart. As He does, He will begin to uncover desires that are out of alignment with His will. Upon your consent, God will restore, renew, and if necessary, redesign your desires. God will affirm integrity in your life and produce evidence of His presence in your life.

S — Success or Significance

In the simplest terms, success is when you add value to yourself, while significance is when you add value to others. Success may be a stepping-stone to significance. But significance comes when you change your focus from adding value to yourself to adding value to others. It causes you to reach beyond your comfort zone and to extend yourself in ways that you never thought you would.

Making a direct correlation between success and significance clarifies how the two differ in motive, influence, time, focus, and benefit in the context of relationships.

- ✓ Motives — Because success is focused on moving or achieving personal desires, the motives of success tend to be very selfish. Significance is a shift of motive. It highlights the importance of being in the relationship. The motives are not selfish. Love is not selfish.

- ✓ Focus — The focus of success is self. It asks the question, how can I add value to myself? Significance asks, how can I add value to others? Significance is the result of the process that expands from self to others. Love does not dishonor others.

✓ Influence — When success is your goal, your ability to impact or influence others is limited to self or those who are near. Significance has the potential of unlimited influence. Your desire for a relationship can be all about how you are impacted, or it can be about how the two of you impact one another, or it can be about how you can come together to influence the masses. Love is not self-seeking.

✓ Time — Because success focuses on you, your success is limited to your lifetime. Significance can last for several lifetimes, in that it can include beliefs based in truths that are passed down from generation to generation. Love does not delight in evil but rejoices with the truth.

✓ Benefit — The benefits of success are limited to your feelings of accomplishment. The benefits of significance are unlimited. You are able to celebrate the accomplishment of others. Love never fails.

Outcome- or Process-Focused Relationship

Figuring out what you believe and figuring out what you want is part of determining whether or not you have a desire for an outcome-based or process-based relationship. Every relationship you enter involves a process. The difference between outcome-based and process-focused relationships is your perspective.

An outcome-focused relationship focuses on end results. It mandates that you have clearly defined end goals going into the relationship. There is often an immediate need for status on the relationship. This perspective is sometimes so focused on fulfilling the desire that it does not pay attention to the means by which the desire is filled. If your desired outcome is to not be alone, you may very well find yourself in a relationship strictly for the purpose of not being alone. Are you in love with wanting to be in love?

A process-focused relationship is one in which the focus is on getting to know one another. There is no need for an immediate label on the relationship. The emphasis is enjoying the relationship, peace of mind, and learning whether there are shared beliefs and compatibility of core values. When adversity or challenges arise, they are viewed as an opportunity for growth.

Bringing Your Desires into FOCUS

Your beliefs and core values are changing with time and experience, which means you will need to reflect and figure out what you want in a relationship. What you wanted as a child is not what you want now. Figuring out what you want may take some time, but it is time well spent. Truth be told, some of the greatest lessons you will learn can be learned when you have experienced a break-up. So consider your past relationships and learn what you can from them. You will learn that you don't have to accept what you don't want, which prepares you for what you do want *before* the next relationship starts. Become accountable for where you are in your relationship. Figure out what you want. Think about your past relationships and answer these questions.

1) Was your last relationship an outcome-based relationship or a process-based relationship? What, in retrospect, can you learn about yourself?

_____

_____

_____

_____

_____

_____

2) What was your involvement or contribution to the failure of your last relationship? Was your last relationship based on success in the relationship or significance in the relationship?

_____

_____

_____

_____

_____

_____

3) Do you want to be reactive or responsive? What action will you need to take?

_____

_____

_____

_____

4) How was your past relationship in alignment with God's desire? How was it out of alignment with God's desire?

_____

_____

_____

_____

5) How will writing down your desires impact your future relationship?

_____

_____

_____

_____

CHAPTER 5

Figure Out What's Blocking You

Moving from one relationship to the next does not fix your relationship issues. The issues will move with you because the issue is in you. You can reject or accept that fact. Rejecting it will keep you on the move. Accepting it will free you to move forward.

Rochelle — a Case Study in BS

Rochelle loved her boyfriend more than anything in the world. She would do almost anything for him. They had been dating for almost five years. They had a whirlwind romance, and after only three months of dating, they decided to buy a house and live together. Subsequently, they had two children, and she was pregnant with their third child. Rochelle shared that she wore an engagement ring to make Donnell happy, but they really weren't engaged. Donnell really wanted to get married, but Rochelle didn't feel that they were ready yet. They were working on some trust issues that needed to be resolved. Rochelle reported that she was sure that after she birthed their third child, lost all the weight she'd gained from the three pregnancies, they'd paid off some of the debt, and some family issues calmed down, she would marry Donnell if he asked her to marry him again. She was sure that they would then live "happily ever after."

Rochelle said that the main reason she wanted to wait was because marriage was a big step with a big commitment, and she didn't want to rush into anything prematurely. She had witnessed the arguments and conflicts between her parents, and she was not going to make the same mistake they'd made. She and Donnell were not going to do what her parents had done. Rochelle was serving up a load of BS.

"Then I let it all out; I said, 'I'll make a clean breast of my failures to God.' Suddenly the pressure was gone — my guilt dissolved, my sin disappeared."

Psalm 32: 5 (MSG)

First Things First

The first step to resolving any issue is to acknowledge that there is an issue that needs to be addressed. Your issue is toxic love and unsatisfying relationships. As a result, you have been hurt, you have unmet needs, and you have unresolved issues. I know how that feels, and I can imagine how you are feeling and dealing with all that you have endured. Let me first say, you are stronger than you think you are. You may not feel very strong, but the fact that you are still here, that you are reading these words, is a testimony to your strength.

My hope is that you use your inner strength to figure out what is blocking you from getting what you want. You don't think it's laziness, because you have been consistent in your pursuit of love. You know it's not passion, because you've given all you have to give. So, what is keeping you from the love you want? The acronym OBSTACLES will help you figure out and begin to move beyond your blocks.

OBSTACLES

O — Overwhelm

The first thing I want you to do is to breathe. That's right. Take a deep breath. There is no denying that you are feeling some intense feelings right now and that overcoming the situations in your life seems nearly impossible. You may think that no one else understands what you are going through or what you are feeling. These thoughts are causing you to feel isolated, overwhelmed, and anxious. It is important for you to know that even though your feelings are intense, the strength and power to rise above your circumstances and to get what you want are yours for the having. You may feel lonely, but let me assure you, you are not alone. You have the power to overcome the overwhelm. Here's how to do it.

B — Bring to Light

Every change that you want to make is going to require you to step out of the denial you stepped into because of overwhelming discomfort and pain. When you acknowledge you are operating in denial, you can begin unpacking the emotional baggage you've been carrying. Bringing those emotions out of darkness and into light causes them to lose their power. The first three emotions for you to bring to the light are blame, bitterness, and boasting.

Blaming may be how you are manipulating your relationships. Assigning the responsibility of a wrong to someone else allows you to express your feelings without accepting responsibility for your actions and feelings. While this may seem to help you feel better in the short term, it positions you in the seat of powerlessness.

Blaming often partners up with bitterness, which is a stagnant form of hidden anger and resentment. Bitterness is like a cancer that grows out of your refusal to let go when someone or something is taken from you. That will be explained in more depth in the "L" of OBSTACLES.

Boasting is when you take pride in your own achievements, which is fine so long as it does not become grandiose. When you are talking too much about your accomplishments, you may be protecting yourself by attempting to make yourself feel better and look like more than you are. Boasting may be your attempt to put on a mask so you don't have to deal with the things you don't want to deal with, or it may be a tactic to distract others in hopes they will not see the areas where you feel incompetent or vulnerable.

S — Shine More Light

You may think that there is no need for you to acknowledge your issues, but if you do not address them, you will continue to do exactly what you're doing and get the same result. Pain, loneliness, and powerlessness are not what you want, so you need to be honest about where you are. So, shine some more light. Consider if shame, self-pity, and selfishness are negatively impacting you.

While blaming says that you have done something bad, shaming tells you that you *are* something bad. If shaming was a major factor in your emotional growth process, you were encouraged to feel that negative circumstances were a result of your behavior and character. If shaming was part of your history, operating in perfection, being a people pleaser, attacking or striking out at other people, and withdrawing from the real world to live in a fantasy world may be part of your story.

Self-pity is an attitude that establishes you as the subject of every offense, injustice, indignity, and injury. It is a pattern of thinking that leads you to operate in hopelessness, self-destructive behavior, and/or excessive self-comfort. If self-pity is part of your BS, it means your inner critic demeans you by constantly repeating your poor decisions, mistakes, and injustices you've experienced until you embody the errors you made and become one with them.

Last but not least is the issue of selfishness. Behaving selfishly means you have stopped considering the impact your decisions and behaviors might have on those around you because you are more focused on protecting yourself or having your needs met — even if it takes away from another or hurts them. If you feel as though you have sacrificed your own needs too often (unmet needs), selfishness will cause you to refuse to put yourself in that type of position again.

This is not an exhaustive list of BS, nor is it an exhaustive list of how BS shows itself or impacts your life. It is given to you to help you begin to understand the mindset and attitudes that have negatively impacted your life, interrupting your ability to focus your mind.

T — Truth

Truth is the light that dismantles the BS. Speaking the Scriptures gives you the energy you need to reprogram your thought process, beliefs, and attitude. Truth does not stop you from feeling the bumps, potholes, curves, and swerves of the road, but it will keep you steady, safe, and secure during the journey. Scriptures are the truth that changed my thoughts. When you speak the truth, you begin to erase your negative thoughts and feelings. Truth helps you understand your identity and your worth. I encourage you to find a few Scriptures that speak to your heart and spirit, reminding you of who God says you are.

A — Accountability

Moving beyond your obstacles requires that you become accountable. Allow me to share with you a short story about accountability from author and pastor John Maxwell:

"Once upon a time there was a noun named Accountability, the precious offspring of Love. Without anyone to hold accountable, Accountability sought Wisdom and learned that it's not good to be alone. Now operating in true purpose, Accountability enjoyed the life-changing understanding of esteeming others better than itself. Accountability began to hold others accountable, as well as teaching the value of striving together in unity and helping others to do the same."

Accountability is the practice of being accountable. For you to be accountable means that you accept responsibility for and are prepared to give an explanation for the congruence or incongruence of your walk and talk. God has made a provision in which each of us can give an account for our words and actions. Take time to find a female who is willing to serve as a coach, and at least one to serve as an accountability partner. Your coach should be someone who prompts you to grow closer to the Lord and walk in integrity. She should have wisdom gained through her choice to align her beliefs, thoughts, and behaviors so her life brings forth diamonds instead of coal. She should be able to question, challenge, encourage, and admonish you. Your accountability partner can be someone who, like you, is learning about the journey to living an irresistible life.

Accountability to God is another dimension of accountability. In Jesus Christ, God has given us an advocate to translate our words and speak on our behalf. What a blessing this is. This means you can have a conversation with Jesus, letting Him know your thoughts and feelings, and He will translate it to the Father. You don't have to worry about if you are, or are not using the right words, because Jesus knows the intentions of your heart. When you share with Jesus, Jesus shares with you. This creates space and opportunity for agreement on performance, mutual respect, clarity on goals, effective communication, and commitment to continuous personal growth! Now, doesn't that sound yummy?

The gift of having an accountability partner is an added blessing, in that the right partnership provides clarity of vision and more than one set of eyes can see the same end. Having an accountability partner will help keep you focused, on track, and celebrating sooner. Confessing to and talking with God heals your spirit from the wounds of sin. Confessing to and praying with an accountability partner heals the wounds of your soul. God gave you His Son and sisters to help you be accountable.

C — Christ

The love, compassion, patience, and power of Christ are the guarantee for transformation. How well do you know Him? I'm not talking about you going to church. How well do you *know* Him, His thoughts, and His desires? Establish an intimate relationship with the One who loves you and cannot fail. Before you seek to be in a relationship with another imperfect human being, be intentional about getting to know Jesus the Christ. Your entire life will change as soon as you acknowledge your inability to produce the experience of love you desire and invite Him into your life to teach you about love. A relationship with Him is a relationship you can bank on, because His love is perfect and it never fails.

L — Let Go

You say you want to move forward and experience a relationship filled with passion and purpose. In order for you to do that, you are going to have to let go of the negative baggage from your history. If you hold onto the offenses of your past, they will take away the joy, peace, and happiness of everyday living. It can negatively impact your health and every good thing that comes into your life. Letting go, also known as forgiving, releases you from being bound to your past. Making the decision to let go of the hurt, anger, betrayal, injustice, etc. is much easier said than done.

You will definitely need to ask Christ to help you with this part of the process. You will also need to rely heavily upon Him so that unforgiveness doesn't creep back in. It takes a while for the fruit of forgiveness to grow and mature.

E — Engage

Facing your obstacles is going to cause you to experience a myriad of emotions. Please, do not try to escape or deny your feelings. You may not know why you experience certain emotions, but engage them. Suppressing and ignoring your emotions has been a large part of your relationship challenges. Allow yourself to feel, to cry, to vent, etc. You will find that having that accountability partner is really useful when you are engaging your memories and emotions. She will be there to help you process them.

S — Surrender

Surrendering is another component you may struggle with. It is difficult to relinquish your control, considering all you have endured. But when you confess that you have been avoiding confrontation and running from your past, when you confess your fears, your reluctance, your anxiety, and your shortcomings, you create space and opportunity for God to step in and do it His way. Have you ever seen the bumper sticker that reads, "Jesus is my co-pilot"? If this has been your approach, perhaps you should switch seats and allow Jesus to take the wheel. Think about it. If you had the power to produce the relationship you want, you would already be loving and living it. The fact that you don't have it means you need help. So surrender. Let it go and let God take control.

Bringing Your Obstacles into FOCUS

Following the steps of the acronym will help you identify your obstacles. Once you have them identified, you make the space for God to come in and do a work in you. He will begin to heal your unhealed hurts, meet your unmet needs, and give you the insight you need to resolve the issues that need to be resolved. Making the decision to step out of denial may very well be one of the most difficult decisions you make. Trust the Lord, His wisdom, timing, and methodology.

1) Take care of first things first. Confess your faults, feelings, and fears to God by writing them down. Ask God to guide you through this process. Once you have a list written, give it to God.

_____

_____

_____

_____

_____

_____

_____

2) What is your commitment to this journey?

_____

_____

_____

_____

3) What are you going to do when past failures, fear, and anxiety arise and attempt to prevent you from moving forward?

_____

_____

_____

_____

4) What is your greatest fear when it comes to stepping out of denial?

_____

_____

_____

_____

5) Stepping out of denial is difficult. What is your motivation to step out of denial? What will happen if you remain in denial?

_____

_____

_____

_____

_____

_____

CHAPTER 6

Observe

Observing is the more than looking at something or someone. Observing is the ability to actually see what you are looking at.

W hen talking about diamonds, a color evaluation is done to determine how colorless the stone is. The less color, the higher the quality and the more valuable the stone is considered. When considering your love life, one of the Four Cs is coloring. It is important for you to know what you are using to color your choices. This being said, Chapters 6, 7 and 8 are written to help you optimize through observation. Take time to see what is coloring your choices. Choices colored with the Word of God are purer, resulting in relationships of higher quality and of greater value.

Can't See for Looking

Janet was in a good place in her life. She was about to graduate from college, her internship was going well, she had a promising career ahead, and she was in a relationship with Jason, who was a good man. She was doing a lot, but she thought she could handle it. Why then, with everything going so well and being in order, was she feeling so overwhelmed? Finals were approaching, and she could hardly focus on anything.

When Janet slowed down and looked at her life, she realized that her relationship was the source of her overwhelm. She had to be honest with herself. She realized that she and her boyfriend had gotten together a few months before graduation and that the major reason was that "all" their friends were leaving the university in pairs.

It might not have been so bad if they had kept the relationship platonic, but to prove that their relationship was real, they soon started sleeping together. He had even begun talking about post-graduation living arrangements. This was too much for Janet. Things between them were getting too serious and moving too fast.

She did not want to upset her boyfriend. He was really a good man. So, she wore a façade of happiness, which in turn only made things worse. Identifying the source of her emotions enabled Janet to deal with her feelings. She was able to share with her boyfriend that she needed the relationship to slow down. Jason wasn't happy with her request. However, he did honor it.

"Do not remember the former things, or ponder the things of the past. Listen carefully, I am about to do a new thing, now it will spring forth; Will you not be aware of it? I will even put a road in the wilderness, rivers in the desert."

Isaiah 43: 18-19 (AMP)

Becoming Aware

Your commitment to take this journey has demonstrated your strength and desire to find and experience true love. So far, you have taken time to figure out your beliefs, you are gaining clarity on your wants and desire, and you have begun to figure out what is blocking you from moving forward. Now, it is time for you to go a bit deeper. It's time to stop looking outward and backward, and begin doing some careful and intentional looking inward. When you spend too much time looking outward, you give power to external forces. When too much time is spent focused on, and thinking about your past, you end up living in your past and missing out what is happening today. When you take time to intentionally observe your beliefs, desires, and thoughts, you gain insight about why you are doing what you are doing and why you are feeling what you are feeling. This insight helps you understand where you are emotionally, psychologically, spiritually, and physically, and allows you to live in the "now". The acronym OBSERVE provides seven areas where awareness will benefit you in life and love.

OBSERVE

O — Overwhelmed

Overcoming overwhelm is such a large part of the FOCUS Framework that it merits being fleshed out some more. Doubt, uncertainty, insecurity, and being mentally unprepared are all contributors to feeling overwhelmed within a relationship. They drain you of a lot of energy, mentally and psychologically at first, and then physically. Though feeling overwhelmed is an emotion, it originates in the mind, not the heart. It often occurs when your mind attaches your current thoughts to events and emotions of the past and causes you to imagine possibilities, possibilities that produce fear. In the story above, Janet's feelings of being overwhelmed were not a result of final examinations or of the demands of her internship; they emerged from what she thought about the fast pace of her developing relationship. Once she was able to narrow that down, she was able to focus on the challenge and come up with a solution. Focusing your attention on the moment, without judgment or attachment to preconceived outcome, will help you overcome your feelings of overwhelm.

If you are feeling overwhelmed, slow down and observe what is going on in your life and in the world around you. What is drawing from you mentally, emotionally, and physically? Are you experiencing doubt, uncertainty, or insecurity? Are you mentally unprepared for something you are engaging in? Answering these questions empowers you to address the issue and overcome being overwhelmed.

B — Behavior

You may think that observing your behavior is somewhat of a waste of time. However, it is a wonderful way to verify what your core values and fundamental beliefs are. You have already taken the time to figure out what you believe. Now you want to take time to ensure that your behavior is in alignment with your beliefs. Don't be surprised if you find that some of your behaviors do not align with your beliefs. For instance, you may have discovered that you believe that men are supposed to be protectors and providers. However, you hear yourself telling your man that he doesn't have to protect or provide for you because you can do it for yourself. Granted, you can indeed protect and provide for yourself. In fact, your saying those words is a form of protection. However, when you are in a relationship with a man, your behavior should be in alignment with your beliefs. If they are not, you will experience dis-ease in your soul and spirit.

S — Speaking

Hear the words that are coming out of your mouth. Your words have power. If you say you are lonely, your ears will hear your voice and summon the emotions of loneliness. Pay attention to the words you are speaking. Be aware of what you are speaking and releasing into the world. This is also a good time for you to begin speaking truth and victory over your life. Speak out loud. Hearing your voice will activate your faith, strengthen your beliefs, impact your behavior, and change your life. Speaking the word of God guarantees results, because His word always does what He intends for it to do.

E — Emptiness

One of the worst feelings is being in a relationship and feeling alone and empty. You may have entered into a relationship as an attempt to escape emptiness, only to find out that being in a relationship did not fill the void, it made you more aware of it. Emptiness is the remnant of a wounded heart. It is the feeling you get in your heart and soul when you want to be connected with someone, but connection is not available. Unhealed hurts, unmet needs, and/or unresolved issues are dark, suppressed places where emptiness lives. Joy and sadness, pain and pleasure, emptiness and fulfillment — they are all housed in your heart. When you lock the door on any one of them, you lock the door on all of them. Awareness is the key to unlocking your heart. Once it is unlocked, you will be able to connect with your feelings.

R — Resentment

According to Merriam-Webster, resentment is a feeling of indignant displeasure or persistent ill will toward something regarded as a wrong, insult, or injury. I like to keep it simple. Resentment is when you think about what someone said or did that hurt you, and that memory sends you back to the moment and the feeling. You are continually *re-sent* to the incident of injury. Resentment keeps you stuck in the past, which means you cannot live in the now. Resentment can act like an emotional cancer if it is repressed and allowed to fester. The odds of you enjoying a long-term, true love, passionate relationship are stacked against you so long as resentment is present. The good news is that observation creates awareness. Your awareness is your frontline defense to eradicating resentment, because you can make the decision to live in the present, not in the past.

V — Victimized Mentality

It is likely that you have been the victim of an offense or injustice. If you choose to view your life through the filter of being a victim, you are operating with this mentality. "It's not my fault. They [or it] did it to me," and "If it weren't for him I wouldn't be ___" are phrases you are speaking. Operating as a victim, you are blaming outside sources rather than acknowledging your responsibility for your actions.

Another major impact of operating with a victimized mentality is the feeling of powerlessness. Because feeling powerless doesn't feel good, you'll find yourself projecting and blaming someone or something for causing that feeling. Being the victim causes you to perceive yourself as unable to do anything about your circumstances, giving others the power over your life. The feeling is debilitating in that it undermines your attempts to do anything about your situation. In a relationship, this translates to thoughts that include never getting what you want, not being able to trust your significant other because you feel he is out to get you, and that life is difficult — so difficult that no one will understand what you are going through.

The faulty belief system of victimization will make you think everything is complicated and there is nothing you can do about it. Once you begin to change your belief system, you begin to regain the power and the authority over your life. You are able to do this through Christ. He is the One that strengthens and gives you power.

E — Escape

Escape, or living in your own fantasy world, is the final area we will observe. One way you may be dealing with pain, problems, phobias, and patterns of thinking and behaving is by trying to escape or hide from them. Escape can be achieved through substances like drugs and alcohol. Yet these are not the only means of escaping. Avoidance, food, love, shopping, relationships, and sex can also be used as forms of escape.

Attempts to escape are draining and futile. It's like running from your shadow in a wide-open field on a sunny day. There is no getting away from it. It may show up at a different angle, but it follows you wherever you go. The only way to escape is to find shade or cover. So that's what you do. You keep your hurts, hangups, and habits covered, throw shade, and limit your ability to fully engage in relationship.

The deeper your pain, the greater your temptation to escape. But in *1 Corinthians 10:13 (AMP),* the word of God says, "*No temptation [regardless of its source] has overtaken or enticed you that is not common to human experience [nor is any temptation unusual or beyond human resistance]; but God is faithful [to His word—He is compassionate and trustworthy], and He will not let you be tempted beyond your ability [to resist], but along with the temptation He [has in the past and is now and] will [always] provide the way out as well, so that you will be able to endure it [without yielding, and will overcome temptation with joy].* " In other words, when you trust your life into God's care, He's got you. God will never leave you; He'll never let you be pushed past your limit; He'll always be there to help you come through it — you are not alone.

Bringing Your Observations into FOCUS

Observing your situation and being honest about how you have been approaching life may be a rude awakening. Let me first assure you that all of us sleepwalk through life to some degree. Waking up is a decision, a decision you will need to make on a daily and sometimes even hourly basis. It is a decision that has less to do with your ability to live anew and more to do with your *determination* to live anew. As long as you have the determination to wake up and change your life, the Holy Spirit provides you with the ability.

Observing your situation should open your eyes to the truth that you are powerless to transform your life. If you had the power to change your life, you probably would have changed it by now. Even though you are powerless to change your life, you do, however, have the power you need to turn your life over to the One who has the power. When you admit to God that you are powerless to transform your life and ask Him to empower you by sharing

His power with you, you will begin to perceive the new thing God is doing in you!

Take a moment to observe. Are you feeling overwhelmed, empty, victimized, or resentful? Are blame and selfishness evident in your relationships? Do you spend your energy trying to escape? If the answer to any of these is yes, do not be discouraged. Admit your powerlessness to God so you can regain power.

1) Which of the modes discussed above best describes how you are approaching and abiding in love and life? Be specific.

_____

_____

_____

_____

2) What is moving through life in this mode costing you?

_____

_____

_____

_____

_____

3) Are you ready to change your relationships and your life by changing the way you think and behave?

_____

_____

_____

_____

4) How will you gain the power to change?

_____

_____

_____

_____

CHAPTER 7

Openness

People are always looking for open doors and new opportunities. But the truth is that the greatest opportunities are found behind the hardest door to open — the door of a closed mind. Don't give up on opening your mind. Once you open it, you'll begin experiencing life to the fullest.

Opening the Door

Anika was smart, sensitive, and had a great sense of humor. She appeared confident to those who knew her in the work place. The way she walked exuded confidence. She was concise and consistent in her decision making. She had a way with clients. Her charisma had allowed her to seize opportunities and advance in the company. She was described as the type of person who went above and beyond the call of duty. And it was paying off: She had just received some good news. She'd been offered and accepted the position of partner at the law firm. She couldn't wait to share her good news with Bob, her significant other. Her dream was coming true. Now, if she only get her home life together, everything would be great.

Anika sat before me with a sadness that could be read on her face and in her body language. She was sad because Bob had not responded to the news of her promotion in the way she thought he should. Yes, he had said he was happy for her, but something about his response seemed disingenuous. When she brought this to his attention, he simply responded that he was happy for her, but he was disappointed that she had not discussed her intentions to accept the position with him before making her decision. He went on and on about how they were supposed to be a team and how major decisions should be mutually made, and yada, yada, yada. Anika was not really listening to him, she was too busy formulating her defense, which by the way he made mention of. She couldn't believe he had actually made a comment about her treating their home like a courthouse and their bedroom more like a courtroom. What did he expect? She was being who she was and doing what she did. She was not going to change, so he was going to have to learn to deal with it.

> "The beginning of wisdom is this: Get [skillful and godly] wisdom [it is preeminent]! And with all your acquiring, get understanding [actively seek spiritual discernment, mature comprehension, and logical interpretation]."
>
> Proverbs 4: 7 (AMP)

Open Up for What?

Needing to change, wanting to change, and being open to change are three different things. They are intrinsically related to one another and are the succession of a process that precedes voluntary change. This is where orientation or alignment comes into play. By now, you realize that you need to change. You may even have the desire to change. But until you open your mind, your heart, and your spirit to the love you so deeply desire, the change you need and desire will not happen. Only you can decide if you want your life to produce coal or diamonds.

See, it is nearly impossible to receive what you do not believe. Let's say you meet a guy named Joe. You can tell Joe that you are not interested in his advances, but if he is not open to hearing what you are saying, he will not believe you. When you don't answer his call, he'll send a text. When you ask him not to call or text, he will not receive your important tidbit of news and will continue to call and pursue you. Whether the information is positive or negative, you have to be open to it before you understand it and honor it.

When you were younger, your willingness to be open subjected you to negativity and positivity. A child who grows up in a shame-based, emotionally dishonest or spiritually and emotionally hostile environment builds a wall of defense and relates differently than a child who is raised in a nurturing, supportive household. How that child relates should not be judged as right or wrong. That child is coping with his or her situation the best way he or she knows how.

Over time, you have developed coping mechanisms, mechanisms that have served you up until now. Now, however, is the season to open up and take an objective look to see if the walls you built to protect yourself as a child to keep yourself safe are the same walls that keep others at bay.

Until you are intentional about opening your mind, heart, and spirit to healing and all the possibilities that come along with it, your unhealed hurts, unresolved issues, and unmet needs will continue to negatively impact your relationships. Through observation, you have come into the knowledge of how you came through. Now is your time to understand where you've come to. God did not bring you this far to abandon you. By believing He is able to heal your broken heart, meet your unmet needs, and resolve your unresolved issues, you can begin to receive the healing and restoration that has been prepared for you. Working the steps presented in the acronym OPEN will help you to open up, positioning you to experience the irresistible.

OPEN the Eyes of My Heart and Soul

O — Overthrow Secrecy

Alcoholics Anonymous has a saying: "You're only as sick as your secrets." This doesn't mean your life should be an open book in the public library. It does mean that any secret you are keeping that is causing harm to you or to someone else should be shared with God and to someone you trust. Disclosing secrets enables your healing process to begin. It helps you to be accountable for your words and actions, making it harder to continue the harmful behavior.

The truth is that tending to wounds of your heart, soul, and spirit is no different than tending to wounds of the body, in that the only way for the infection to be removed is to open the wound and clean it out. I can imagine that you are already wincing. Everything in you is probably saying, "Don't do it!" Anticipating the discomfort is understandable, but the process is necessary. In time, the discomfort will decrease and you will begin to heal.

Openness to change provides the environment for healing. When you open your heart and your mind to God, shame loses its power. You see, God loves you in spite of your shortcomings, failures, and flaws. God knows what you have done, what you have endured, who you are, and the difference between the three. He will help you learn the difference, as well. He has provided forgiveness for the wrongs, mercy for your shortcomings, and grace for it all. The big question here is your willingness and ability to believe and receive the forgiveness provided for you. What are you struggling with from your past and in your present? The next section will hopefully help you to open up.

P — Place All Your Trust in God

Asking someone with trust issues to place all their trust in God may seem a bit strange, but that is the next step. You will need to place all of your trust in God. This requires you to go deep down in your heart, the part of your heart that does not operate from a place of reason. Placing your trust in God means that you are going to stop trying to figure out everything on your own.

You have already spent time figuring out what you believe, what you want, and what is stopping you. Now, in order to experience transformation, you have to let God do a work inside of you. Don't assume that you know it all. Consult God about everything, not just the "spiritual" things, not just the "big" things, everything. Listen for His voice in everything you do. Allow Him to lead you everywhere you go and in everything you do. Developing trust is a matter of developing a relationship. Don't run away from God. Run towards Him.

E — Expect and Embrace Change

You have been asked to open your mouth and confess. You have been asked to open your eyes to observe. Now, you are being asked to open one of the most difficult areas of all: your mind. In order to embrace change, you will need to expect change, and expecting change is a state of mind. If your mind is closed to change, change will not happen, because when it shows up, you will reject it. The most difficult thing to open is a closed mind. So, how do you open a closed mind? You humbly accept the Word of God.

God's Word tells us to get rid of all uncleanness and all that remains of wickedness, and with a humble spirit receive the word of God, which is implanted, actually rooted in your heart. Toxic love has tainted your mind, will, and emotions, but the Word of God is able to save your soul. When you believe and receive the Word of God, you believe you can cast your cares upon Him because He cares for you. When you open up and give God your burdens, the burdens you are carrying automatically lighten because they are being shared. And trust me. No matter how heavy your load is, God can handle the heaviness.

N — Not for Them, for You

It is important that your desire comes from an internal place and not from external pressure, that your change is for you, not for them. Someone else will benefit from your change, but healing and wholeness is a state of being that you must want for yourself. The change needs to be for you because the transformation will happen in you. Changing for anyone other than yourself sets you up for instability and powerlessness. Your desire for change should not be for parents, children, or lovers. When you live like this, you will have to change every time the "they" or "he" in your life changes. And what happens when "they" or "he" is no longer in your life? Your commitment to open up needs to be to yourself and for yourself.

Your intellect will tell you that opening up to God is okay, but opening up to another person — that does not compute. Every defense in your psyche will sound warning alarms. After all, some of the deepest wounds you have were caused by people you thought you could trust. This is why you have to renew your mind daily. It is will not be enough for you to read through this book one time and expect total, complete, and irreversible healing to occur and be maintained. You will have to continue to read the word of God so that you can counter all of the negativity in the world.

Bringing Your Openness into FOCUS

Your mind is a battlefield. Cultivating and maintaining an open mind is going to be an intentional and ongoing process. Only an unwise person goes into battle without a coach and a strategy. Your strategy is to implement the Four Cs. Open your thought process for the purpose of gaining clarity. Use the clarity to help you discern what is coloring and influencing your thoughts, attitudes, and behaviors. Once you knowing what is coloring your thoughts, attitudes, and behaviors, you can choose what to keep, and decide what is not serving you and needs to be released. The more you implement the Four Cs process, the more efficient, thorough, and specific you will be in cultivating and maintaining a strong defensive and offensive strategy of openness. Having a coach improves your ability to be objective and open. Having someone who has experience in this arena of battle gives you an advantage when implementing your strategy. Answer these questions as a mind-opening exercise.

1) What do you believe about God? Who is God? How does God feel about you? What has God done for you? What is God doing in you?

_____

_____

_____

_____

_____

2) What part of being open causes you to be anxious? How come? How will you counter the anxiety?

_____

_____

_____

_____

_____

3) What secret(s) are you hiding? It may be a personal secret or a family secret.

_____

_____

_____

_____

4) What is your motivation for FOCUSing? Why is now the time for you to FOCUS? Who are you doing it for?

_____

_____

_____

_____

5) Other than God, who is the person you will trust and share this secret with?

_____

_____

_____

_____

CHAPTER 8

Obey: A Dreaded Four-Letter Word

Obey is a four-letter word despised by many and enjoyed by few. Obeying is not a matter of submitting to rules that restrict you; it's a matter of voluntarily ascribing to principles that take the limits off of love and life.

Obey? Say What?

Keisha was anxious and worried. "What ifs" and "if onlys" were guiding her life. What if they didn't have enough money to pay the bills? What if they had car trouble while they were on vacation? If they could have left at noon instead of 12:15, they could have avoided the traffic. If she had been born in

August instead of September then she could have started kindergarten earlier and could have graduated from high school at the age of 17. Keisha lived in a perpetual state of regret and self-induced anxiety. Her anxiety level was so high that you could actually hear the tremor in her voice and see it in her hands. As she put it, she was a nervous wreck. And what made it worse was that her significant other, David, was not in the least bit worried about anything. His calm demeanor really put Keisha off. How could he be so calm when there was so much that could go wrong? David was always telling her to calm down, that she worried too much, and that everything would work out. But Keisha was certain that somebody needed to worry and they needed to be doing something. She didn't want to look back and see that things could be different if she had only.…

What Keisha had yet to learn was that if she would trust God and obey, she could and would begin to experience peace. Introducing Keisha to the serenity prayer was a benchmark in her transformation. When she grasped that she was not expected to be in control of every outcome, a burden was lifted from her shoulders. She was finally able to stop living a life based on performance and begin living a life centered on being, being in the presence of God, being obedient to God, and being reliant on God.

> *"But now that you've found you don't have to listen to sin tell you what to do, and have discovered the delight of listening to God telling you, what a surprise! A whole, healed, put-together life right now, with more and more of life on the way!"*
>
> Romans 6: 22 (MSG)

Who Are You Telling to Obey?

I know that this four-letter word carries as much potency as some other four-letter words, but it is not intended to insult you. Obeying is a concept that is rejected in 21st-century western culture. Yet, Scripture says that obedience is better than sacrifice. God wants you to listen to Him! It's not because He has a big ego. It's because He knows what He has prepared for you, and He knows what's best for you. So, before you make the choice to skip this chapter, take a few minutes to read the words that are written on these pages. You may be able to see how resisting obedience to God is not working for you.

God does not speak to you just so He can hear His own voice. God speaks to you because He loves you and wants to protect you, guide you, and provide for you. Not listening to God negatively impacts every aspect of your life. When you go Frank Sinatra on God and "do it your way," you are telling God that you know better than He does. You are usurping His authority and trying to be a mini-god. Failure to obey often initiates confusion, delay, and unnecessary drama. Living a life of obedience provides the shelter of God. Operating in disobedience, whether it's operating outside of the will or timing of God, is like moving out from under the shelter. You may not notice it immediately, but over time, overexposure to the elements, be they sun, rain, or hail, can be harmful to you. Why not enjoy the shelter being supplied to you? You are the one who will prosper.

Obeying God is not necessarily popular, but it is definitely prosperous. When you do what you want to do, you get the results that you can produce. When you do what God says to do, you get God results. And according to *Jeremiah 29:11*, the results of

God's plan for you includes prosperity and are filled with hope and a future. If obeying God is good for you, why is it so difficult to do? Volumes have been and could be written on the difficulties of being obedient to God. But rather than focusing on the challenges, let's focus on a solution. You can develop a lifestyle where trusting and obeying are your norm. The acronym OBEY will help you practice these four steps to prosperous living.

OBEY

O — One Day at a Time

Understand this: You didn't get where you are overnight, and your transformation will not happen overnight. Transformation is a process, and processes take time! Your thought patterns, character defects, and negative habits didn't develop in one day, and they won't be removed in one day. In some cases, it has taken you a lifetime to develop into the person you are, and it will take the rest of your life to be transformed. Renewing the mind is an everyday process — and it is most achievable when it is approached from the perspective of one day at a time.

Living one day at a time means not judging yourself based on your past and not stressing yourself out on the possibilities of tomorrow. Living one day at a time is about you learning how to live in the now. Living in the now is trusting God to be with you where you are now, to provide what you need now, and to give you instructions for now.

B — Be Still and Know

Only God knows, in totality, what you were created for, how you were knit together (*Psalm 139:13*), what the future holds, and how it's all going to work together. You would think that as a human being, *being* would be easier. Being is one of the more difficult tasks in life. Nevertheless, there is something inside of you that needs to be reminded that you don't have to "do" something about everything. There are times you need to be still and know that God is God. Here are a few areas you can profit in by *being*:

✓ **Be still in your emotions.** Being emotionally alert helps you process your emotions rather than trying to escape intense negative feelings. Comfort eating, going to night clubs, even procrastination are all forms of emotional escape. Allowing yourself to feel and process your feelings promotes health and wholeness. Know that God is sharing your suffering and He will see you through.

✓ **Be spiritually sensitive.** God has a time and a season for everything. You may be trying to fool yourself in the minute-by-minute choices you make. There have been times when you have good intentions; unfortunately, they never amount to anything measurable or tangible. Good intentions without the coupling of supportive behavior does not yield the desired results. There is a gap between your intentions and your actions. This is the space I want you to focus on. It is in this gap that your "self" operates. You, yourself, could be undermining your progress by justifying your behavior of not following through, of not closing the gap. Being still in the gap is to operate on the power and in the timing of God, knowing that He can and will do in you and through you what He said He would do.

✓ **Be humble.** Trusting and obeying God requires you to be humble. Being still in humility is a matter of you not thinking you are higher than or better than anyone else. It is not pretending or putting forth any false illusions of lowliness. Be aware of what you are doing. When you do or say things solely for the purpose of gaining acceptance or affection for yourself by persuasive and subtle flattery, you are operating in false humility. Think about your relationships. Were you more interested in entering into debate than into a dialogue? Did you listen to your significant other for the purpose of giving him advice, or did you listen because you had a genuine loving interest and wanted to share, learn, and grow in his experience? If you can relate to either of those examples, false humility is at work. False humility tears down rather than builds up; it apologizes but does not seek the benefit of change.

✓ **Be willing to be who God says you are.** When you are traveling a familiar road and it is riddled with potholes, do you risk damaging your vehicle by driving on the road because it's familiar, or do you find a new route? If you self-sabotage, you continue driving the same route and try to fix the potholes while you drive. Pay attention to your behavior. Are you attempting to fix your mistakes by top-loading them with increasingly bad decisions? At what point do you allow God to be in control? Know your triggers and your limitations. You don't have to prove how strong you are to anyone, not even to yourself. Remember, when you admit that you are weak, you extend God an invitation to be strong. You are uniquely made by God. There is no one else created exactly like you. So be willing to be the one-of-a-kind, God-designed, custom-made you.

E - Expect to Fall Short

Self-sabotage is not an act, it's a process: a complex, tragic process that pits people against their own thoughts and impulses.

It will tell you that a set-back is a failure and a failure is the end. Heed this warning. Expect to experience set-backs. In fact, you can utilize your set-backs as set-ups for comebacks when you have a plan of accountability, confession, and appropriate response. Be prepared to fall, so you can fall forward. Give all you have, be your best, and expect that there will be times when you will be imperfect. Expect your imperfections to resurface from time to time. Expect that temptations will present and sometimes they will win. Falling short is part of the human experience; you will fall short. When you do, and you will, do not beat yourself up or condemn yourself. Confess your weakness, get up, and begin again.

Y — Yield Your Will to the Will of God

Give way to God's way! You have tried your way and come to the realization that it is not working for you. So how about doing something different today? Today is a new day, filled with new mercy and great grace! Today you can make the choice to bind your mind to the mind of Christ and yield your will to the will of God. You will have to make this choice every day, sometimes multiple times a day. When you choose to align your will with God's, you are making the choice to trust, obey, and experience the abundance of life that comes through living in relationship with God and the freedom He has provided for you. In the early part of this process, your will is going to want to yield to your emotions — pride, self-pity, low self-image, feelings of unworthiness, fear, doubt, and/or anger. It will try to negate the process and your progress. Don't listen to the hype! Instead, yield your will to the will of God and allow God to complete the work He began in you.

Bring Your Ability to Obey into FOCUS

Obeying may not provide you with as much clarity as you want, but it will bring to the forefront many of the issues that have been coloring your life experience, as well as thoughts, attitudes, and behaviors you may need to cut. As you practice the process of living one day at a time, of being still and knowing that God is God, of expecting to fall and preparing to get up, and of yielding your will to the will of God, you will find that the benefits of obeying God far outweigh the perceived restraints of being obedient.

1) Consider obedience from this perspective: Obedience to God is not a limitation to do only what God says do. Obedience is the freedom to not have to do what sin mandates you do. Does this statement change your perspective of obedience? How?

---

2) How do you get in your own way? What can you do to prevent self-sabotage, especially in love and relationship?

_____

_____

_____

_____

3) How will living one day at a time impact you? Your relationships?

_____

_____

_____

_____

4) How will the mercy and grace of God impact your decision to yield your will to God today? Each day?

_____

_____

_____

_____

CHAPTER 9

Confront

No matter how hard you try to avoid confrontation, the inevitable truth is that confrontation cannot be avoided. Either you will live from the offensive line and confront your past, or you will live defensively because your past is confronting you.

Throughout life you are faced with a myriad of choices, choices that shape your life. What is considered a small choice can have a major impact, changing the course of your life and impacting your entire future. Just as a diamond cutter has to choose the best way to minimize loss and maximize yield when choosing in which shape to cut a rough diamond, you will have to make loss and yield choices as you journey to irresistible life. You will find

Chapters 9, 10, and 11 to be instrumental in helping you make wise decisions, optimize your experiences, and emerge with brilliance. God does not waste one single hurt. He will use your past experiences to equip you for your current reality. You can do this.

The Courage to Confront

Leslie had been isolated from her family and her friends. She was financially and emotionally dependent on her fiancé, Steven. She was alone in a strange country and didn't even know how to speak the language. Leaving Steven at that moment in time did not seem like the most logical thing to do, yet somehow, she knew that it was the right time to confront him. She asked Steven to take her to the airport with a plan to return home to the States. He taunted and teased her about not being smart enough to navigate her way home, about not having the money to go home. He called her stupid for saying she was leaving. After all, he was the best thing that had ever happened to her. Tears streamed down Leslie's face. Then Steven said something that boosted her courage. He said that if she left him, she would regret it. He would call off the wedding and she would never hear from him again. Leslie knew he was telling the truth. She knew he would create some story in which she would be the villain and he was the one who left her. Leslie knew this was her opportunity to leave. She, again, asked him if he was going to take her to the airport. He agreed.

Steven laughed all the way to the airport. He belittled her as he walked with her to the ticket counter. When they got to the ticket counter, he spoke on her behalf, telling the agent, "My fiancée wants a one-way ticket back home, but she doesn't have any money and I am not paying for it. Can you all help her out?"

Leslie remembers the look on the agent's face. Even more vivid in her memory is the look on Steven's face as she took money from her wallet and gave it to the agent. It had taken her over a year to secretly save up the money to buy her ticket. It had taken her more than five years to gather the courage to confront her greatest fears. What would people think? She was going to be alone. But she had finally done it. She had just taken her first step towards freedom.

"When the Philistine rose and came forward to meet David, David ran quickly toward the battle line to meet the Philistine."

1 Samuel 17: 48 (AMP)

Coming Face to Face

One of the most important questions you need to ask yourself at this point is if you want to be made whole? It may seem like a pretty dumb question, but it's not. It is a choice you have to make. There are those who want to be irresistible and there are those who are in love with the *idea* of being irresistible. Before you stand face to face to confront your Goliath, you need to know which outcome you want. It's like in *John 5*, where the man had been lying beside the pool for 40 years waiting for someone to put him into the water for healing when the water was stirred. Finally, one day, Jesus asks him if he wants to be made whole. You would think that was a no-brainer type question. It was definitely a yes or no question. But this man's response was not a yes or a no. He starts talking about how "what had happened was...." Dreaming and talking about wholeness while lying on a mat was one thing, but wholeness would require him to pick up his bed and walk. So just to ensure that you really want to FOCUS, that you are ready to change, and that becoming irresistible is really what you want, the question must be asked: Is irresistibility what you really want? If so, it means you can't hang out with the complainers, or party with pitiful. It means that you will have to confront your past.

See, so far, your past has been confronting and conforming you. The negative memories and painful feelings have determined how you have navigated your way through love, relationships, and life. You have cried, you have complained, you've lashed out, and you've hidden, but now it's time for you to confront the events and emotions of your past so that they no longer have power over you. It is time for you to use your power of choice in a way that frames your life for the good.

Confrontation takes courage. Fear may be telling you that you don't you have the courage you need. However, after you look at how courage is gathered, you will realize you are ready to confront the demons of your past. Working the concepts of the acronym CONFRONT will strengthen your faith so you can operate with courage.

CONFRONT

C — Confidence in God

Your ability to confront needs to be rooted in the foundation greater, larger, and mightier than you. Anything less will not provide you with the courage you need. See, when you place your confidence in yourself, you are limited by your knowledge, experiences, and imagination. This is the result of placing your confidence in any human being. But when you put your confidence in God, you can boldly step out, knowing that the same God who created the heavens and the earth, and the same God who brought you through your past, is the same God who will be with you as you move forward. Having confidence in God is a matter of you believing that God is with you and that God is able.

I can understand how your past could cause you to feel like God abandoned you somewhere along the way. You may be asking where God was when you were being abandoned or abused. It may seem like you were alone and abandoned and that the prayers went unanswered and the tears went unnoticed. Let me assure you that you are not alone in feeling that way. As someone who has lived through darkness and abuse, I can in retrospect say that God was with me. This gives me the confidence to say to that though you may not sense His presence, God is with you during your darkest days and during the most painful hours. And it is because He has been with you and has carried and kept you that you are here today.

O — Operating in Faith

Confronting requires you add faith to your fear so you can move forward in courage. It is the decision to actively participate in what God says even though you can't see it, in order to see what God said. You will have to make the choice to act on what God says about you instead of acting on the negative things that have been said about you. Operating in faith is making the choice to stop reacting to the bad that others have done to you and begin responding to the good God has done for you and what the Holy Spirit wants to do in and through you.

One of the challenges with operating in faith is that faith rarely conforms to the parameters of logic and reason. If it did, you wouldn't have to utilize faith. So, don't get distracted by what you see or don't see. Know what God wants for you, receive what God has for you, and do what God says to do, and you will find yourself taking steps of faith.

N — Nipping Fear in Its Bud

Doubt and anxiety, left unattended, will grow and blossom into full-fledged fear, so it's best to nip it in the bud. Fear will tell you any lie to keep you from moving forward. It wants you to remain on the sidelines while your past masters your present and nullifies your future. The courage to confront requires you to get in front of the con. Get in front of the lie with the truth of God's Word. Get in front of the darkness with the light of God's love. You are fearfully and wonderfully made in the image of God. A masterpiece of His craftsmanship. A unique and irreplaceable vessel created to love and be loved. Stop letting the con front you. Get in front of the con!

F — Face Your Past Despite Your Feelings

By now, you may be feeling some strong feelings. After all, you are passionate, sensitive, and emotionally intelligent, and you aren't going to let anyone take that away from you. And you shouldn't. But you also cannot afford to let those things block you from your healing and restoration. When gathering the courage to confront your past, you will experience a multitude of feelings.

When Leslie requested to be taken to the airport, she was feeling fear because she didn't know how Steven was going to react and she didn't know what her future held. She was experiencing sadness and anger. Sadness because her relationship of six years was ending, and anger because she had given six years of her life to someone who didn't love her. She was excited because she was taking back her life, energized because she was experiencing power, and happy because she was doing something for herself.

Don't be afraid to feel your feelings. Feeling your feelings means that your heart and soul are viable, not hardened. Use the years of suppressed feelings as energy to help you overcome. Connect with your accountability partner. She can listen as you process through your feelings, and her presence will help you be *respond-able* and not do anything rash. You are confronting thoughts and feelings, not people. Let your tears flow; let your nose run. Scream, shout, let it all out, and use the feelings of your past to fuel your courage to confront.

R — Release Regret

Again, you have a choice. You can choose to focus on your past with distress and grief, or you can focus on what you have. "What do I have now?" I'm glad you asked. A long-term, non-judgmental, loving, and passionate relationship is what you want, right? Well, a long-term, non-judgmental, loving, and passionate relationship with God is what you have, at least from God's vantage point. God does not regret loving you. Unfortunately, if you choose to hold onto the distress of your past experiences, you will not be able to fully embrace the joy of your current experience. The most successful way to release regret is to grab hold of something else. Reach out, take hold of, and hold tightly to God's love, grace, mercy, forgiveness, etc. Hang onto God's promises, and you will let go of distress.

O — Occupy Your Mind

Now, you may think confronting is about giving someone a piece of your mind. It's not. And I strongly advice that you not do it. You're going to need that piece of your mind at some point in the future. Rather than give your mind away, fill your mind, and meditate on things that are true, noble, reputable, authentic, compelling, and gracious. Think about the best, not the worst. Think about the beautiful, not the ugly. Courage is a behavior birthed from a thought process, not from emotions. Think about things that are praiseworthy, instead of things that make you want to curse. When you occupy your mind with God thoughts, your behavior will reflect and rely on the goodness of God.

N — Nourish the Truth

There is a story told within the Native American community about two wolves, one bad, one good. These two wolves live inside of every person, and they are always fighting with one another to be in control. The question is, which wolf wins the fight? The answer: the one you feed, because it will be stronger.

Truth and reality are at war in your heart, mind, and spirit. Reality wants you to believe that what you have experienced is all you ever will experience, that you are unworthy, that you are overwhelmed, etc. Truth wants you to know that you are tremendously loved, empowered, and have a future. Will reality or truth win the fight? It depends on which one you feed. Feed the truth.

T — Trust that You Are Equipped

When David was on his way to confront Goliath, Saul tried to get David to wear his armor. David put on Saul's armor, but took it off because he was not used to it. Instead, he picked up five smooth stones as his weapon. To Goliath, David and his stones looked insignificant. What Goliath didn't realize was that God was with David. You need to know that you already have what you need to successfully confront your past. You have faith, insight, victory, experience, and wisdom. Most importantly, you have God on your side. You don't need to get anxious or stressed out. All your past experiences have prepared you for this moment. You are equipped. With God you, can do this.

Bringing Your Confrontation into FOCUS

The next chapter will go into more detail on how to use your past experiences to confront and conquer your past. For now, choose a time during your adulthood that you successfully faced something that caused you fear or discomfort.

1) In what or whom had you placed your confidence?

_____

_____

_____

_____

2) What role did faith play?

_____

_____

_____

_____

3) Were doubt and fear present? How did you overcome them?

_____

_____

_____

_____

4) What conversation(s) did you have?

_____

_____

_____

_____

5) Did you have second thoughts? If so, how did you deal with them?

_____

_____

_____

_____

6) How did you prepare your mind?

_____

_____

_____

_____

7) What did you do?

_____

_____

_____

_____

8) How did you know it was the right time?

_____

_____

_____

_____

The answers to these questions are your "smooth stones." Hold onto them. You will need them in the next chapter.

CHAPTER 10

Commence

Every end is a beginning and every beginning is an end. So, what determines if you are beginning or ending? Your perspective. Are you looking back at your past or forward, towards your future?

I Can't Catch Air

As a coach, I often meet clients when they are in crisis. This was the case for Cassie when we met one warm December afternoon. "I can't catch air. My life is totally messed up." These are the exact words Cassie said to me while sitting on the sofa in her living room. "I can't eat. I can't sleep. I can't do anything right. My mind is messed up." Cassie was crumbling under the pressures of her current life and the burden of her past. It was difficult for her to complete a sentence, because she was having difficulty completing a thought. Our conversation allowed Cassie the opportunity to slow down and organize the chaos of her thoughts and emotions. The outcome of our conversation was that Cassie would write things down to help diminish the overwhelm and do an inventory to help her sort out her feelings.

The initial suggestion of doing an inventory was accepted by Cassie but not embraced. She agreed to work on it in 30-minute increments three times during the week. When I checked in with her, she reported that she had not begun. Further conversation revealed that Cassie had only agreed to do the inventory because I had said I thought it would help, and she didn't want to disappoint me. Cassie needed to understand that it would only help if *she* thought it would help, and her focus was to be on herself, not on me. She also disclosed that she was afraid to begin. She was afraid to feel her feelings and preferred to let bygones be bygones. With guidance and encouragement, Cassie began the process of her inventory, and to her surprise, she began to experience freedom from the bondage of her past. It wasn't comfortable, but it was worth it.

> "In the beginning, God created the heavens and the earth. Now the earth was formless and empty, darkness was over the surface of the deep, and the Spirit of God was hovering over the waters. And God said, 'Let there be light,' and there was light."
>
> Genesis 1: 1-3 (NIV)

Bringing Darkness to Light

In the Beginning, the earth was dark, empty, and unrecognizable. It was not until God spoke into the atmosphere that change began to occur. By the end of the working period, transformation had occurred. Time and seasons were in order. Emptiness had been filled. Darkness and light filled their respective places. Nothing was wasted; everything that was fulfilled a purpose.

It's most likely easier for you to accept and understand the good experiences of your life. The negative and dark experiences are not easy to accept or understand. And to be honest with you, some things you will never understand. But even if you cannot understand it all, you can choose to accept that all of your experiences will come together to serve a fruitful purpose in your life, and that now is your season.

During this chapter, you will gain insight on how to bring the darkness to light and lay it out so that God can speak into your life. It will be a bit like mining coal. Your hands will most likely get dirty as you dig into the depths of your past. Your eyes may tear up and your nose may run, but don't let that stop you. The particles of your past may cause you to experience difficulty breathing as they are exposed, but if you stick with the process, you will begin to experience change. Over time, you will experience transformation and the diamond that is buried deep inside will be revealed.

The five-step process you will use to bring your darkness to light is an inventory called INSIDE. Following the instructions provided in the acronym INSIDE will require you to reach inside of yourself so you can gain insight and clarity on the coloring and choices that have impacted your life. Have you been going through life wearing dark shades, or rose-colored glasses? What is tinting and tainting your ability to experience the love and life you want? These are questions you have been asking, but you have yet to get the answers you need. It's time to stop looking outside of yourself for the answers you hold within. It's time for you to go INSIDE.

INSIDE

I — Identify Individuals: Column #1

In this column, list the names of the individual events or people you resent, fear, or have issue with. Start with your earliest or most pronounced memory. You may remember words spoken or left unspoken. You may remember deeds done or left undone. You may or may not think that it is major, but if it comes to mind, write it down. This is a list of offenses and offenders. It may be one word like Adam, milkshake, or red dress.

N — Note the Incident: Column #2

In this column, you are going to list the specific words and actions of the individual person and the specific details of the event listed in column one. What did Adam say or fail to say? What were the details surrounding the milkshake or red dress incident? Be as detailed as you can. This may cause you pain and discomfort, but the more details you bring out of the darkness, the fewer details there are fighting to have power, because darkness brought to light loses its power. If you need support, reach out to your coach. She will support you, not fix or judge you. If your emotions begin to whelm up, don't wait until you are overwhelmed. Utilize the support of your accountability partner.

S — State the Impact: Column #3

Just as Newton's third law of physics says that for every action, there is an equal and opposite reaction, life's laws of interaction state that for every incident, there is impact. This column is for writing down how specific, wounding words or actions affected your life in the past and how they continue to affect it in the present.

For example, let's say that as a child you were not allowed to voice your opinion. You were constantly told to be quiet; you were to be seen and not heard. As a result, while in the presence of adults you had internal dialogues to which they were not privy, and then you went to your room and let your stuffed animals have a piece of your mind.

You're an adult now, but you still don't express your opinion. While in the presence of authoritative figures, you have internal conversations to which no one is privy, and when you arrive in your safe place (home or a specific relationship), you let them have a piece of your mind. Every incident has an impact. It may be negative or positive, but an impact has been made. Write it down.

I — Investigate the Injury: Column #4

You are a triadic being composed of body, soul (mind, will, and emotions), and spirit. The impacts of life either injure or inform your body, soul, and spirit. In this column, you will write down how your basic instincts were injured by a negative experience or informed by a positive experience.

1) Security instincts — how have your body, soul, and spirit been injured or informed when it comes to trusting and feeling safe? Do you operate in freedom or in extreme apprehension and fear?

2) Sexual instincts — how have your body, soul, and spirit been injured or informed when in regard to connecting deeply and engaging with and responding to intimacy?

3) Social instincts — how has your ability to interact with others and follow the group's behavior on a physical, emotional, and spiritual level been injured or informed?

4) Survival instincts — how have your body, soul, and spirit been injured or informed when it comes to your survival instincts? What do you do when you feel threatened, rejected, or angry?

Note: remember there is no hurt that God cannot heal; no burden God cannot lift; no need God cannot satisfy; no issue God cannot resolve; no sorrow God cannot turn to joy.

"and provide for those who grieve in Zion– to bestow on them a crown of beauty instead of ashes, the oil of joy instead of mourning, and a garment of praise instead of a spirit of despair. They will be called oaks of righteousness, a planting of the Lord for the display of his splendor."

Isaiah 61: 3 (NIV)

D — Determine the Imprint: Column #5

An imprint is a mark made by pressure. In this section of the inventory, you will consider what lasting marks the individual, the incident, the impact, and the injury have made on your thought process and behavior process. Experiences of your childhood made an emotional, psychological, spiritual, and physical imprint on you, impacting your approach and contributing to subsequent experiences.

E — Eliminate the Erroneous

The following four points do not go in a column on your inventory, but they are instrumental in your healing process. They will help to clear up erroneous beliefs. Please, take the time to read them. If you need to write them down so they can process from head, to heart, to hand — then write them down. Do whatever you need to do to in order to embrace these truths.

Truth #1: Abuse is never the fault of the one being abused. Abuse is always a wrong behavioral decision on the part of the abuser. Doing this inventory should reveal to you and release you from the untruth that your being abused was your fault. You are not at fault. Yes, an individual violated you; the impact, incident, and injury occurred; and the enemy would have you believe the imprint of guilt. But the inventory is written and the verdict is in, and you are found not guilty. In fact, how about you write that in the Imprint column. Write it in all caps: "I AM NOT GUILTY." Begin to celebrate your newfound freedom from fault.

Truth #2: Maintaining balance is extremely important as you are doing your inventory. Make sure that for every negative experience you inventory, you inventory a positive experience. You will use the same format. The only difference in the chart set-up is found in column #4. When you are recording a negative experience, the heading will be "Injury." When you are recording a positive experience, the heading will be "Informed."

Truth #3: There are five "I's" in the Inventory Process, but there are no "I's" in team. You will not receive the full benefit of the inventory process if you do not have a team. Be sure to identify one person who has gone through the process you are going through (that's your coach) and at least one person who is willing to support you, not judge or fix you, as you go through the process (that's an accountability partner). It is perfectly acceptable to have different accountability partners for different aspects of your healing.

Truth #4: Prayer is essential to your restoration process. Pray alone. Pray with your coach and accountability partner(s). According to *James 5:16*, when you *"confess your sins to one another [your false steps, your offenses], and pray for one another, you are healed and restored. The heartfelt and persistent prayer of a righteous man (believer) can accomplish much [when put into action and made effective by God—it is dynamic and can have tremendous power]."* (AMP) So, pray out loud and pray silently. Pray the Word of God. It always accomplishes what it is sent forward to do and never comes back void.

Bringing Your Inventory into FOCUS

Before you begin this portion of the process, I encourage you to do three things: pray, get some paper and a pen (or a computer), and pray. Prayer is your way of reminding yourself that you are not alone. God is with you. It also fortifies your heart, soul, and spirit. If you are honest with yourself in doing the inventory, you will face the good, the bad, and the ugly of your life. Stay in conversation with God throughout the process. The paper and pen is for, you guessed it, writing. The inventory is a written exercise. Writing (or typing) helps to organize your thoughts. I have provided an INSIDE Inventory sheet for you. You can download it at www.makemeirresistible.com.

If you begin to get overwhelmed during this process, remember these two things. First and foremost, you are not alone. God is with you, and the relationship you are developing with Him is enough to see you through this. Second, you are developing trust-filled relationships with your coach and accountability partner. Your coach can guide you with the valuable wisdom she gained through her experience, and your accountability partner is walking the process with you. Their support will encourage and remind you that in Christ, you are able. Third, when you go inside of yourself and bring the darkness to light, darkness loses its power over you. So, even though it may be painful and unnerving, utilize your resources to push past the pain. Exercise your power by doing the inventory.

It is commencement time, which means it is time to begin experiencing the freedom, peace, happiness, and love you want. This is your gift to yourself. Don't let anything or anyone distract or delay you! Don't say you will start tomorrow. Start today.

CHAPTER 11

Conquer

*You cannot conquer
what you will not
confront.*

Coached to Conquer

Renee's intentions had been to complete her inventory before she met with her coach, but it seemed that every time over the past few weeks when she had sat down to write, something had come up. Either her phone would ring, or she would end up needing to handle some other aspect of life. She had two days left before her scheduled meeting and she had nothing on paper. After struggling internally, Renee did something that she had been avoiding: she called her coach. Her intention was to cancel the meeting. She had procrastinated on making the call because she didn't want to hear a lecture about the need to do her inventory or commitment. She already knew that she needed to do it. She was just having challenges getting started.

To her surprise, the phone call ended up being exactly what she needed. There was no lecture, no judgment, and no pressure. Her coach listened to her fears and concerns, supported her as she explored her feelings, and encouraged her. She realized that her hesitation was based in her unwillingness to sit in her feelings. When Renee hung up the phone, she was still a little anxious about doing the inventory, yet she felt like she would be able to move through her feelings rather than getting stuck in them. Renee began writing her inventory that night.

> "Yet in all these things we are more than conquerors and gain an overwhelming victory through Him who loved us [so much that He died for us]. For I am convinced [and continue to be convinced — beyond any doubt] that neither death, nor life, nor angels, nor principalities, nor things present and threatening, nor things to come, nor powers, nor height, nor depth, nor any other created thing, will be able to separate us from the [unlimited] love of God, which is in Christ Jesus our Lord."
>
> Romans 8: 37-39 (AMP)

More Than a Conqueror

Conquering any obstacle in your life requires that you focus not on the obstacle but on the outcome. It is inevitable that where your mind goes, your emotions and body will follow. The thought of conquering may be more daunting for you than the actual act of conquering. If you think of the inventory as an obstacle or a challenge too big for you to handle, you sabotage yourself and set yourself up for failure. So how and where do you begin? First, you see yourself as more than a conqueror. See yourself as victorious. Keep the outcome of the inventory in view. See yourself living with your hurts healed, needs met, and issues resolved. Visualize yourself at peace instead of in pieces. Having a vision of the outcome will allow you to conquer the interference of "self" and your past.

Don't get it twisted. I am not suggesting that you live in a fantasy world where everything is coming up roses. You are coming out of denial, not creating new ones. As you are working through your inventory, you will begin to feel emotions that you have suppressed. If you get caught up in your emotions, you will not complete the inventory and you will not conquer your past. You don't want to get trapped in your emotions. Envisioning your new self keeps you focused on moving forward. The acronym CONQUER provides you with tools to ensure your success in completing your inventory and conquering the bitterness that accompanies unmet needs, the pain that accompanies unhealed hurts, and the anger that accompanies unresolved issues.

CONQUER

C — Commit

There will always be something for you to do other than working on your inventory. Whether it is family-related, work-oriented, or church-connected, something will present as more pressing. Even cleaning out the attic, a task you have avoided for 10 years, will suddenly become a priority to you. In order to successfully complete your inventory, you will need to make a time commitment. Schedule time for yourself and don't allow something else to take precedence. You are important. Becoming whole is important. Experiencing love, joy, and peace is important. So make time to work on your inventory.

O — Openly Examine

Now that you have made a commitment of time, you want to use your time wisely. You may be tempted to only write down the "big" things and ignore the "small" things. There is nothing too large or too small for your inventory. If you remember that your first grade teacher drew a big red sad face on your assignment, write it down. The fact that you remember something that happened so many years ago means that it holds significance for you.

You have looked at life through the lens of your past, which, in all honesty, has been tainted by your hurts, hang-ups, and habits. So now it's time to be open. Examine your relationships with God and with others, your dependability, your priorities in life, your goals, your attitude, your motivations, and your integrity. The more you examine, the more you can write. The more you write, the more darkness you expose to light. The more darkness you expose to light, the more freedom you experience.

N — Name the Emotion

Your upbringing may have trained you to believe that saying you are angry or frustrated towards your parents or people in authority is wrong. You may have been taught that you should never say that you feel depressed, hopeless, or confused. But the truth is, when you are feeling an emotion, you should put a name to it. There is power in naming your emotions. Recognizing and naming your emotions reduces the intensity of the emotions and validates your inner self. So stop saying you feel some undefined type of way. Everyone feels some type of way. Sit with your feeling long enough to discover what feeling you're feeling and put a name to it.

Q — Question the Impact

Now that you know some of the areas you can openly examine, it is time to explore further below the surface. One of the ways you can go deeper in your inventory is to use the same approach you used in "openly examine," to take a look at your relationships with God and with others, your dependability, etc. When you answer these who and how questions, you add richness to the impact column of your inventory.

U — Understanding the Cause and Effect

One of the ways your mind has been protecting your body, soul, and spirit is by minimizing how words and events of your past have caused injury. An example of this might be saying that breaking up with your ex really didn't matter to you because you really didn't like him that much anyway. You are attempting to minimize your pain by devaluing your relationship. You liked him enough to be in a relationship with him. Or maybe you grew up saying, "Sticks and stones may break my bones, but names will never hurt me." You were not being honest. You were attempting to protect yourself from the pain of words spoken. Understand the cause and effect of the injury. Once you gain understanding, then and only then will you be equipped to prevent future injury.

E — Exchange

Doing your inventory is more than a tool for change, it is a means for transformation through the great exchange. The great exchange is a result of what Jesus has already done for you and provided for you. Listed below are some of the exchanges recorded in Scripture. Keep this in mind while you are doing the inventory. It will serve as a motivation for you.

- ✓ Jesus exchanged your sin for His righteousness. *2 Corinthians 5:21*

- ✓ Jesus exchanged your sin nature for His divine nature. *Galatians 2:20*

- ✓ Jesus exchanged your position for His position so you could call on His name, the name which carries power and authority. *John 14:13*

- ✓ Jesus exchanged your poverty-stricken life for His abundant life. *John 10:10*

- ✓ Jesus exchanged your sickness and disease with His healing. *1 Peter 2:24*

- ✓ Jesus exchanged the curse of the Law for the blessings of Abraham. *Galatians 3:14-15*

When you exchange and accept the truth instead of lies and negative thinking patterns for positive thoughts, the weeping you endured through the night will turn into joy.

R — Remember

Remember to keep your inventory balanced and to stay connected with your coach and accountability partners. Make sure to list positive individuals, incidents, impacts, insights, and imprints.

And be wise. If your emotions are whelming up, reach out to your coach and teammates. They are there to guide and walk with you.

Bringing Your Conquering into FOCUS

Do not skim through or rush through your inventory. Take your time to methodically work on it. The more you detail you put into your inventory, the more healing you will receive from doing your inventory. The more work you put into it, the more it will work for you. Think of it as your personal *in-vent-story*. Get "In" to it. "Vent" — begin to allow your suppressed emotions to flow, but don't let them rule you. "Story" — by engaging in this process you are actively co-authoring your life story with God, the Author and Finisher of your life. Every word written or typed conquers the stronghold of your past, releasing you to live in the limitless freedom of your Creator.

CHAPTER 12

Understand What You Have

It is difficult to profit from something you don't understand. If the only thing you use your piano for is décor, you miss out on the power of the melody it has the potential to produce. Understand the keyboard, the theory, and the potential, and you can tap into the power of music and compose melodies that impact the spirit.

You are growing in your ability to focus and are moving forward on journey to irresistible love. You have gained knowledge concerning clarity, coloring, and choice. Now it is time to learn how understanding and using what you have learned will impact your relationships. The fourth C of the Four Cs of love and the Four Cs of diamonds is cut. In the world of diamonds, the cut does not refer to the diamond's shape but to a diamond's proportions, symmetry, and polish — in other words, the beauty and brilliance of the diamond.

In the world of the irresistible, cut refers to the dimension, consistency, and finish. Your cuts are determined by your decision to cut out living exclusively in the natural dimension, to cut out inconsistency and develop spiritual consistency, and to cut the thoughts that are contrary to the finished work of Jesus Christ. Just as the cut of a diamond is the most complicated aspect of the diamond, the cuts you will have to make will be challenging. But remember, the cuts determine the brilliance and shine of your experience of true love. Chapters 12 and 13 will focus on equipping you to utilize what you have learned for maximum results. So, stick with the process and know that God is faithful to complete what He began in you.

A Slight Misunderstanding

When I met Rebecca, she was overwhelmed by relationships. She had grown up in a household without a father figure. As an adult, she felt ill-prepared and under-equipped when it came to understanding men and being in relationships. Most of her information had been gathered through experience, but her experiences had left her discouraged and withdrawn. She faulted her father for her broken relationships, her mother for breaking up with her father, and the world for being unjust. Rebecca wanted to love and be loved, but she was completely overwhelmed by the thought of once again opening herself to love and the pain that she felt would come with it. Rebecca was a problem solver, so she decided to do something about it. She went to seminars, read blog posts, and talked to other women about how to catch and keep a man. All of the information, tactics, and calculating were too much for her. Love was too complicated.

When I talked to Rebecca, it was clear that her experience or overwhelm was a result of misunderstanding. Her expectation was that she would have to learn some complicated steps for the process. But the truth was that she already had most of what she needed. What she was lacking was the understanding of what she had.

> *"Then he took his [shepherd's] staff in his hand and chose for himself five smooth stones out of the stream bed, and put them in his shepherd's bag which he had, that is, in his shepherd's pouch. With his sling in his hand, he approached the Philistine."*
>
> *1 Samuel 17: 40 (AMP)*

What's in Your Bag?

When confronting Goliath, David understood that the armor and weapons of Saul were not what he needed. He understood that all he needed was five smooth stones. And so he went to the streambed and picked them up.

Your quest for attracting and maintaining true love requires focus. Part of that focus is the understanding of what you need, what you have, and how to use it. This chapter will address what you need and have. You may think your bag is empty. But you need to know that you have what you need. In *Second Corinthians 12:9,* God tells us that his grace is enough. It is all we need. What is God's grace? The acronym GRACE will help you understand the "five smooth stones" God has given you so you can take down your Goliath.

GRACE

G — Guarantee of Victory

The first stone you have is God's guarantee of victory. That's right! God's grace comes with a guarantee of victory. Through the life, death, and resurrection of Jesus, God has already declared you victorious over sin, death, the grave, worry, loneliness, defeat, poverty of spirit, and the list goes on. When you, by grace through faith, accept the gift of salvation given to you and walk in that grace, you are the recipient of the over 3000 promises of God listed in Scripture. These promises are for you and they are guaranteed, because God's Word never fails.

Understanding that you have the promises of God provides confidence and comfort when confronting your past. With such a vast list, it is impossible to highlight them all in this writing. So I am going to highlight three that are directly related to you becoming irresistible.

✓ You have God's guarantee of perfect love, which means you are saved from destruction. God is love. When you move and live in a life of love, you live in God and God lives in you. Love has the run of the house, becomes at home, and matures in you. You stop worrying, being overly anxious, and living to please people. You begin to understand that your standing in the world is identical with Christ's and that fear doesn't darken your past, overshadow your present, or distort your future. (*John 3:16; 1 John 4:18*)

✓ You have God's guarantee of joy. Having joy means you have the hope and strength to conquer. God is the God of hope. Understanding His hope for you provides you with the fullness of joy. The joy of the Lord is designed to be your strength and stronghold. The awesome thing about joy is that it emerges from an internal source and is not impacted by external stimuli. Joy is activated by your faith, which activates the power of the Holy Spirit. This in turn causes you to abound in hope *and* overflow with confidence in His promises. Get into God. Let God into you and enjoy His gift of joy. (*Nehemiah 8:10; Romans 15:13*)

✓ You have God's guarantee of peace, which is God's gift of wholeness. God's peace provides more than a lack of chaos. It is not limited to a state of tranquility. It encompasses security, safety, prosperity, and contentment. God's peace makes and keeps you safe and prosperous. When you live in the peace of God, you understand that there is nothing missing or lacking in your life, that you have access to the abundance of God. The peace of God surpasses all human understanding. (*John 16:33*)

You have the guarantee of God's love, joy, and peace! You do not need to be afraid. Victory belongs to you!

R — Redemptive Power

Because you have confessed with your mouth that Jesus is Lord and believe in your heart that God raised Him from the dead, your life is within the auspices of the redemptive power of Jesus. What this means for you is that you are no longer who you used to be. You may have done what you did, but you are not defined by what you did! You are a new creature in Christ! Your relationship to God through Jesus Christ wiped your slate clean. Understand that within the redemptive power of Jesus Christ is where you find everything you need. Whether you need healing, reconciliation, restoration, provision, protection, or power, you have it. What does this mean for you? It means that you are able and you are irresistible! (*Romans 10:9; 2 Corinthians 5:17-20*)

A — Acceptance

Accept God's forgiveness. When God forgives you, He totally wipes your slate clean. If your slate has been wiped clean, how come you keep writing negative messages on it? Ask God to help you release the offenses and hold on to His forgiveness. Accepting God's forgiveness is critical in your being able to move forward. See, the time is coming when you will need to forgive. And if you haven't accepted forgiveness from God, there will not be any forgiveness in your heart *for* you to *give*. When you ask for God's forgiveness, receive it. Receiving and giving forgiveness is a gift of God's grace.

C — Comforter

Jesus promised the gift of the Holy Spirit, the Comforter. The Comforter is present to comfort you. So, if you are hurting, rather than run to other sources, how about running to the Comforter? Because so many people are hurting, and hurt people hurt people, seeking comfort from people makes you susceptible to the possibility of being hurt instead of comforted. Even when they mean well, you will find that other people do not have everything needed to comfort you. If you need an advocate, intercessor, or a counselor, call on the Comforter. He will provide the strength, clarity, support, and guidance you need. The Holy Spirit will help you find the answers to your questions, answers that are most likely already inside of you. The Holy Spirit will help you to focus on living in the now while examining the past and gaining a clear vision for the future.

E — Encouragers

God's grace is a gift that encourages us not to give up. By giving us His guarantee of victory, His power of Redemption, the ability to accept and give forgiveness, and the gift of the Comforter, God is encouraging you to keep moving forward towards an abundant life. Jesus came as an example for you so that you could learn the art of focusing and living abundantly. He has provided pioneers who have already paved the way and companions to walk the journey with you. You have everything and everybody that you need for now. As you continue your journey, God will continue to provide based on your needs for that time. Don't worry about what you will need in the future. Trust God and live in His grace.

Bringing Grace into FOCUS

Remember, God's grace is truly sufficient. Everything that goes into living a life that pleases Him, a life that is irresistible to love, has already been given to you through Jesus. God's grace is yours to have. Understand the "stones" of GRACE. Bathe them in the word of God until they become smooth and useful to you. Pick them up and put them in your bag before you confront and conquer your Goliath.

1) What understanding have you gained concerning the guarantee of God's promises? What confusion do you still have?

   _____

   _____

   _____

   _____

2) What understanding have you gained concerning the redemptive power of Jesus? What confusion do you still have?

_____

_____

_____

_____

_____

_____

3) What understanding have you gained concerning accepting an extending forgiveness? What confusion do you still have? Who do you need to forgive? Write down their name(s).

_____

_____

_____

_____

_____

_____

4) What understanding have you gained concerning the Comforter? What confusion do you still have? What do you need the Comforter to help you with today?

_____

_____

_____

_____

5) What understanding have you gained concerning encouragement, and where it comes from? What confusion do you still have?

_____

_____

_____

_____

You want to make sure you get a clear understanding of what God's grace is. You will want to acknowledge and receive the presence and covering of God's grace. If you still have some confusion, enter into a conversation with God. Ask Him to provide you with understanding. He is generous in His giving and will be more than happy to give you clarity, so you can FOCUS.

CHAPTER 13

Using What You Have

*Looking at what you don't have can cause
you not to use what you do have. Start
where you are. Work with what you have.
Trust God to supply your needs.*

Using, Not Abusing

Once Rebecca became aware of what she had, her hope increased. Yet, it was not until she began to use what she had that her feelings of being overwhelmed began to dissipate. She began to apply the principles of GRACE to her life. Her thought process began to change; she no longer saw herself as a victim. Her attitude changed from an attitude of negativity to an attitude of being grateful. Her timidity decreased. She began to smile more. Her relationships blossomed as she became more confident and outgoing.

One day, Rebecca was taking time to reflect on how the grace of God had impacted her life. Her thoughts traveled from her childhood, through adolescence, to adulthood. Somehow, she had always managed to make her way through the darkness. Somehow, someone always managed to cross her path when she was in need. Somehow, though not always the way she wanted, her needs had been met. Rebecca was beginning to understand how, even when she wasn't aware of it, God's grace had always been present in her life. A tear slowly traced down her cheek. The place in her heart that had always felt empty, the longing for a father that had never been met, was being filled and satisfied. Rebecca was experiencing the amazing and irresistible impact of God's grace. She understood what she had, and she understood how to use it.

> "David put his hand into his bag and took out a stone and slung it, and struck the Philistine one his forehead. The stone penetrated his forehead, and he fell face sown on the ground."
>
> 1 Samuel 17: 49 (AMP)

Receiving Grace

When confronting Goliath, David knew what weapons were in his arsenal and he was confident that what he had was sufficient. He understood that even though Goliath was a giant, all he needed was five smooth stones. Why five? It was not because David thought he might miss with one stone and need another. David picked up five stones because Goliath had four brothers. David also made sure that the stones he picked up were smooth. How did they become smooth? Because the consistency of running water has the ability to smooth rocks.

God's Word is alive and moves like running water. The more you use His Word with your God-given gift of grace, the smoother the stones of grace will feel in your hand. Getting comfortable with using God's Word to smooth your stones of grace takes time and practice. So, I want to take this opportunity to make sure you know how to maximize God's grace. This will keep you from becoming frustrated or from abusing the gift you have been given. This being said, Chapter 12 was designed to make sure you have a clear understanding of the truth of God's grace and that He has given you His gift of grace. See, God's grace is not intended to be the kind of gift you receive and put on a shelf or pack up in a closet. It is God's intent that you use, operate in and respond to His gift. This chapter is designed to ensure you know how to use God's gift of grace you have been given.

I am going to use the same acronym of GRACE. Whereas Chapter 12 highlighted the activity of God, in this chapter I will be highlighting your action and response to what God has done for you. I do want to take time to make sure you understand using God's Word and responding to His grace: these are the kinds of things that are more caught than taught. I'll do my best to provide you with information and examples on the how to utilize God's GRACE, so you can maximize the gift. But if what I have written is not something you can grasp onto intellectually, hang in there and follow through. Eventually your spirit will catch it. When it does, you'll find that God's grace is sufficient. As with any gift, you are responsible for how you respond to it and cherish it. Grace is a gift from God; you do not deserve it, nor can you mandate that He give you grace.

GRACE

G — Gain Confidence by Using the Guarantee of Victory

As we discussed in the last chapter, you have the guarantee of victory. But you can resist or receive the guarantee. Receiving it gives you the confidence needed to bring order to chaos, light to darkness, and hope to despair. When you find yourself in the midst of a complicated situation, your natural instinct is to fight or run. If suiting up for the proverbial fight is warranted, put on the full armor of God and stand (*Ephesians 6:10-18*). If making and existing is the answer given by wisdom, then I say in my best Jenny voice from the movie *Forrest Gump*, "Run sister, run." Whichever choice you make, know that you are the winner, and that as the winner you have the privilege and the right to declare your victory according to the Word of God. What does that look like? I'll use the same three examples from Chapter 12.

✓ You are in a showdown with the Goliath of your history. It is telling you that you are unlovable. Remember, you have God's guarantee of love. You can smooth the stones with these words:

✦ God loves me so much that He sent His only Son into the world to save me. God said it. That settles it. I believe and receive it. (adapted from *John 3:16*)

✦ As I look back over my life, I can see how God's love, grace, and mercy have been with me, I believe with deep, consistent faith that God loves me. God is love. I live in God's love, and God's love lives in me, no matter what anyone says. (adapted from *1 John 4:16*)

✓ You are in a showdown with the Goliath of your history. It is telling you that your life will always be a hot mess and you will always be unhappy and depressed. You have God's guarantee of joy.

✦ I am looking at every complicated situation as space and opportunity for God to show up and show His sovereign and miraculous power. Beginning today, a hot mess is an absolute gift. The pressure that comes with it forces my faith into the open and shows its true colors. So, I will not try to get out of anything prematurely. I'm going to let the mess do its work so I will become mature, well-developed, and abundant in my faith. My mess will become my message. God will get the glory! (adapted from *James 1:2-4*)

✦ Today I am wearing the turban of beauty on my head instead of the ashes of mourning. I am nourishing my skin in the oil of joy instead of mourning. Instead of complaining, I am expressing to God my thanksgiving and praise. Through Jesus I am strong and magnificent, distinguished for integrity, justice, and in right standing with God. God created me and through my life, God will be glorified. (adapted from *Isaiah 61:3*)

✓ You are in a showdown with the Goliath of your history. It is telling you that you will always be overwhelmed. You have God's guarantee of peace, which is God's gift of wholeness.

✦ I have the gift of Jesus's perfect peace, not the kind of peace the world gives me. So, there is no need for me to feel abandoned or orphaned. I do not need to be upset or distraught. Lord, let your perfect peace calm me in every circumstance and give me the courage and strength for every challenge I face. (adapted from Isaiah 26:3). *John 14:27, Philippians 4:19,* and *Philippians 4:6-8* are other verses you may find useful.

You have the guarantee of God's love, joy, and peace! You do not need to be afraid. Use what you have. Victory belongs to you!

R — Remember the Redemptive Power of the Cross

You did what you did, but you are not what you have done. Dark forces of the past will repeat negative memories in an attempt to keep you separated from the redemptive power of Jesus Christ. You can avoid a relapse of your thoughts, attitudes, and beliefs by *re-membering*, or reconnecting, yourself to the saving power of Christ Jesus. When Goliath talks BS to you, sling a God-stone back at him by re-attaching your thoughts to the Word of God. Listed below are a few examples.

- ✓ When your past says you will never change, remember the Word of God says you have put off the old man and have put on the new man, which is renewed in the knowledge after the image of Him Who created you (adapted from *Colossians 3:9-10*).

- ✓ When your past says you are a disappointment, remember the Word of God says you are complete in Him Who is the Head of all principality and power (adapted from *Colossians 2:10*).

- ✓ When your past says you are too overwhelmed to be productive, remember that the Word of God says you can have the peace of God that passes all understanding by keeping your mind on Him. You can do all things through the strength of Christ Jesus (adapted from *Philippians 4:7-13*).

A — Approach All Things with Forgiveness

You have the choice to resist or accept God's gift of forgiveness. When you resist God's gift of forgiveness, you make the choice to remain bound to the person or event that wronged you, causing you to remain stuck in the offense. When you accept forgiveness, you accept the gift of freedom from your past. Offering forgiveness has the same effect. When you offer forgiveness, you make the choice to release your offender, which releases you from the bondage of the offense. When you think about it, forgiveness is a powerful tool of liberation. Because part of being irresistible is living a life of liberation, approach all things with a willingness to forgive and live in the freedom of forgiveness.

Ephesians 4:31-32 (NIV) provides words to smooth your stone of forgiveness. It reads, *"Get rid of all bitterness, rage and anger, brawling and slander, along with every form of malice. Be kind and compassionate to one another, forgiving each other, just as in Christ God forgave you."* Other words to smooth your stone of forgiveness can be found in *Matthew 6:14-15*, and *Luke 6:38*.

C — Communicate with the Comforter

All of us have what I like to call a knower. You have one. Your knower warns you of danger and gives you instructions. You may call it your first mind or simply say, "Something told me…." That something, that inner voice, is the voice of the Holy Spirit. Spending quiet time with a focus on hearing your inner voice will alert you to situations that may lead you into harm's way or draw you away from God's will for our life. Be intentional about making time to learn how to hear the Holy Spirit's voice and learn to listen to your Knower. Scriptures to help you smooth this stone:

> "For all who are allowing themselves to be led by the Spirit of God are sons of God. For you have not received a spirit of slavery leading again to fear [of God's judgment], but you have received the Spirit of adoption as sons [the Spirit producing sonship] by which we [joyfully] cry, "Abba! Father!" The Spirit Himself testifies and confirms together with our spirit [assuring us] that we [believers] are children of God."
>
> Romans 8: 14-16 (AMP)

E — Encouragers

Encouragement is not a one-time experience. It is something you will need every day, multiple times a day, and some days more than others. You will need to be intentional about giving and receiving the encouragement you need. Make and keep an encouragement plan. Keep Scriptures on your cell phone or posted on post-it notes, and set an alarm so you don't forget to be encouraged.

When you are face with temptation, the Words of *1 Corinthians 10:13 (NIV)* provide strength:

> "No temptation has overtaken you except what is common to mankind. And God is faithful; he will not let you be tempted beyond what you can bear. But when you are tempted, he will also provide a way out so that you can endure it."

Philippians 4:6-7 is good for counteracting anxiety, as is *Psalm 9:9*. There is a Scripture to help you through every situation. Search and find the Scriptures that speak to your situation.

Bringing the Use of Grace into FOCUS

Remember, God's grace is truly sufficient. Everything that goes into living a life that pleases Him, a life that is irresistible to love, has already been given to you through Jesus. God's grace is yours to have. Understand the stones of GRACE. Bathe them in the word of God until they become smooth and useful to you. Pick them up and put them in your bag before you confront and conquer your Goliath. Remember *2 Peter 1:3*.

1) Make a list of the "Goliaths" in your life. What Scripture will you use to take each one of them down?

_____

_____

_____

_____

2) What lies have you allowed to define your character? What truths, "I am" statements, will you replace the lies with?

_____

_____

_____

_____

3) What will you do to ensure you are accountable for your words, attitudes, and behaviors? How will you utilize your accountability partner(s)? Be specific.

_____

_____

_____

_____

_____

_____

_____

4) How will you utilize your coach? Be specific.

_____

_____

_____

_____

_____

_____

_____

5) Write down your strategy for staying encouraged.

_____

_____

_____

_____

_____

_____

Remember, the stones David used were smooth. The more you use the Word of God over your stones, the smoother they will become.

CHAPTER 14

Stand

The ultimate test of strength is not found in how skilled you are at tearing someone down with your words or actions. The ultimate test of strength is displayed in your ability to stand firm when all hell is breaking loose around you and bricks are being thrown at you.

Let God Be God

Marie was concerned, and rightly so. The incidents of abuse were escalating in frequency and intensity. Leo had not hurt her physically, but his verbal attack was effective. During the day, he belittled her constantly. During the night, he wouldn't allow her sleep as he quoted scriptures into the early morning hours. Marie's exhaustion was beginning to impact her work performance. Mounted on Leo's verbal attack was the now occasional destruction of property. Marie occasionally found pictures, clothing items, and household items shredded. She knew that it was only a matter of time before the physical violence turned toward her, so she didn't want to approach him in a way that would agitate him. She turned to God in prayer and confided in a close friend that she trusted. Marie and her friend prayed together. They prayed continually, asking God to intervene and to provide wisdom, courage, and strength. Two things happened.

First, God provided Leo with a night job. This allowed Marie to get her much-needed sleep. The second event happened one morning when Marie woke up and was sitting on the side of her bed. She had the distinct impression in her spirit that the day had come. Leo was going to have to leave. To her surprise, she was calm and confident. She sat in the same position until he came into the bedroom. She didn't have the words to say what she needed to say, so she sat and prayed. Leo came in and greeted her. She said, "Good morning," and then before she could talk herself out of it, she told Leo that their relationship was not good for either of them and that she thought it best for him to move out. Leo turned towards her. He looked her in the eyes and said, "If I leave, I'm not coming back." Within two days, Leo had packed his belongings and moved out.

> "Therefore, put on the complete armor of God,
> so that you will be able to [successfully] resist and
> stand your ground in the evil day [of danger], and
> having done everything [that the crisis demands],
> to stand firm [in your place, fully prepared,
> immoveable, victorious]."
>
> Ephesians 6: 13 (AMP)

Stand Still

One of the difficult aspects encountered during reconciliation, renewal, and restoration is knowing when to be still and let God be God. Gaining strength and courage will begin to motivate you to want to do something to change your circumstances and the people around you, when really, what God is focusing on is changing you. The Message Bible does a very good job of laying it out and making it plain. It reads:

> *"Be prepared. You're up against far more than you can handle on your own. Take all the help you can get, every weapon God has issued, so that when it's all over but the shouting you'll still be on your feet. Truth, righteousness, peace, faith, and salvation are more than words. Learn how to apply them. You'll need them throughout your life. God's Word is an indispensable weapon. In the same way, prayer is essential in this ongoing warfare. Pray hard and long. Pray for your brothers and sisters. Keep your eyes open. Keep each other's spirits up so that no one falls behind or drops out."*
>
> Ephesians 6: 13-18 (MSG)

Learning how to STAND is the beginning of the final phase of FOCUSing.

STAND

S — Share Challenges and Victories

A lot of emphasis has already been put on your need to share your challenges with your coach and your accountability partner(s), because that is a large part of the process. FOCUSing is also about keeping balance, so don't just share the challenges and setbacks, be sure to share your accomplishments and victories. Becoming irresistible is a journey, not a destination. Have an attitude of gratitude. Thank God for the transformation you are experiencing. Rejoice and celebrate along the way.

T — Make Time, Take Time

As you begin to experience healing and wholeness, you may very well drift away from the practices that helped you along the way. In order to stand firm, you will need to review the five keys of FOCUSing until they become your way of life. Making time and taking time on a daily basis to filter your thoughts, feelings, beliefs, and actions through the five keys of FOCUS will help you to stand firm in your wholeness. You will most likely have to cut off some relationships, activities, and people. That is part of the process. Make and take time daily to review your day. Failure to do so may allow you to fall back into your old mindset and habits. So, pause, pray, and focus again.

A — "A Game," Bring It On

By this phase of the journey, you should be beginning to enjoy peace. You may find yourself smiling and laughing more. It's like a burden has been lifted from your shoulders. For sure, you want to celebrate the transformation occurring in your life. At the same time, you don't get complacent in your progress. Commit to bringing your "A game" every day. Admit, Apologize, and make Amends. Admitting your wrong thoughts, attitude, and actions is the act of owning your responsibility in the situation and being accountable. When you make a mistake or cause someone insult or injury, admit you're in error or have given offense to yourself, to God, and to another. Doing so releases you from guilt, blame, and shame.

Apologizing is the second phase of this process. "I'm sorry" is not an apology. An apology is the act of explaining the cause of your behavior. When you apologize, you explain the underlying reason for your action. It includes an explanation of your thought process, attitude, behavior, and motive.

The third and final phase of this process is making amends. Making amends is about doing what is in your power to mend the relationship. It's more than you giving lip service. When you make amends, your goal is to restore justice through your words and actions. Amends are about a genuine change in your behavior.

Bringing your "A game" benefits you and the person you bring it to. Remember, when forgiving and making amends, you cannot control the other person's response. Your responsibility is to do all you can do to repair any negative impact you caused. After you have done that, all you are required to do is stand.

N — Note Your Progress

There will always be people in your life and voices in your head trying to convince you that they know you, that you are no different, and that you will never change. If you are not deliberate about taking note of the changes you are experiencing, you may just believe them. No matter how small they seem, make note of your progress. Note that you are in a process and you are making progress. You may not be where you hope to be, but you certainly are not where you were. (Woohoo!) God is doing a continual work in you, and He is faithful to complete the good work He began in you. (*Philippians 1:6*)

D — Do a Focus Test

Doing a focus test allows you to stay stand firm in the changes God is making in you. It will allow you to:

- ✓ **F** — be aware of your **f**eelings, so you are not operating in denial

- ✓ **O** — monitor your **o**penness to change, wrongdoings and forgiveness

- ✓ **C** — **c**heck your belief systems

- ✓ **U** — **u**nderstand your strengths and weakness so you know your greatest areas for potential growth

- ✓ **S** — **s**ettle down, so you can hear from God with clarity

Bringing Your Stance into FOCUS

Diamonds in the raw are valuable. However, when you want to place a diamond in a setting, the diamond shows best if it has been processed. That's the only way its brilliance is going to shine through. Clarity, color, choice, and cut are recorded ratings that determine the brilliance of the diamond. Creating a format for your daily FOCUS provides a structure or a setting for your brilliance to shine through. If you want your life to be irresistible — that is, a life filled with attracting positive energy, impacting your sphere, and experiencing true love for years to come — take your stance. You are free to create your own format for daily FOCUS or you are welcome to use the FOCUS checklist provided for you at makemeirresistible.com.

CHAPTER 15

Stay Focused; RESPECT Yourself

Gaining the respect of others doesn't happen just because you tell them to respect you. Respect is a choice. You can choose to become distracted by the drama and complications of insisting that everyone show you respect at all times, or you can choose to stay focused and respect yourself.

Wait for It

t was 6:50 pm on January 12, 2017, and Janice was still waiting on her ride. She was livid. How many times was she going to have to tell Jeff that if he drove her car while she was at work, he would have to pick her up from work on time? She had reiterated that very fact this morning right before he kissed her goodbye. He had said he would be waiting on her. She had clocked out at 5:15pm, fifteen minutes later than she had told him to be there. She figured that would give him some leeway. But 6:30? Come on. At 6:47 pm, she'd decided to call him for the fifth time. Again, no answer. He wasn't responding to the text messages either.

This was the third time this month he had left her waiting. Janice had done her best to school him on respect. He had promised he wasn't going to be late again. This was the last time she was going to let him use her car. If he was going to be her man, he was going to have to learn to respect her and her stuff.

> *"Do you not know that your body is the temple*
> *of the Holy Spirit, who is in you, whom you have*
> *[received as a gift] from God, and that you are not*
> *your own [property]."*
>
> 1 Corinthians 6: 19 (AMP)

Give Me Just a Little Bit

You are well on your way to becoming irresistible. You are resisting the lies, negativity, and darkness. You are beginning to grasp how beautiful, valuable, and wonderful you are. One of the challenges you may be encountering is that people from your past may not be able to see the changes God is doing inside of you. That may be because sometimes it takes internal change time to manifest externally, or it could because acknowledging the changes in you makes them too uncomfortable. In either case, don't sweat it. Stay focused and respect yourself. The acronym RESPECT will help you focus your energy on esteeming yourself.

RESPECT

R — Realize and Recognize

Don't be deceived. Realize that BS will reemerge, and that slipping back into your old mindset, attitude, and behavior patterns can happen before you know it. Recognize your triggers. Holidays and significant events are peak season for BS relapse. You don't want to be alone during Christmas or Valentine's Day, so you go out and get a "holiday beau." No one serious, just someone to pass the time with. Or you choose not to get a beau, and now the voices in your head are replaying a message of unlovable, undesirable, and unworthy. Recognize and be prepared. Keep your five smooth stones close and ready. Put your full reliance in God, reserve time every day for Bible study, and stay connected to your accountability partners and your coach.

E — Embrace the Change

You have overcome fear and exercised courage to get to where you are today. Do not allow anyone to diminish your progress or criticize your change. The temptation to go back to your old ways will be real. After all, you are more comfortable with them because you lived with them for longer. Don't beat yourself up because you experience or possibly fall subject to the temptation. Instead, understand temptation for what it is: a challenge to battle. Keep your focus on embracing the changes you are experiencing and your victory.

Give the battle to the Lord. Let Him fight it. As the young folk would say, "Ain't nobody got time for that." Spend your time and energy on embracing how your fear to confront is shifting to the courage to conquer, and on how your propensity to react is maturing into the ability to respond. Embrace how your feelings of inferiority are diminishing and your confidence in Christ is increasing. The more you embrace and settle into your transformation, the more you will enjoy living life!

S — Slow Your Roll

Don't jump just yet. You don't want your desire to be irresistible to others to be so strong that you prematurely jump into a relationship before becoming totally irresistible to yourself. Timing is paramount. If you don't have time for a conversation with God, you don't need to have a conversation with "John Doe." If you don't have time to spend with God, you don't have the time to spend with "Joe Blow." Wait on God's timing. Impatience is a fruit that grows from the root of pride. Pride wants you to think you have things under control. When you get to the point when you think you can do it on your own, you are likely at the point of needing help. Remember, you don't have control of your life until you willingly give your control over to God.

Oh, and one more thing. If you think you "need" a man, you need to slow your roll. You don't need to have a man in your life until you don't "need" a man in your life. Being in a relationship should not be the means for you experiencing wholeness and contentment in your life. So, slow your roll and focus. It is when two whole people come together that the two experience a wholesome relationship. Make sure you allow time for God to restore, renew, and make you whole. Focus is a continual process. Process takes time. Love is patient. Let patience do its perfect work.

P — Prioritize

Put first things first. Irresistibility comes from God. Do not resist God. Put God first. Know what is most important to you. God, family, serving others, physical health, knowledge, peace, rest, work — figure out the order of priority. Prioritizing provides a framework for making plans and moving forward. *Proverbs 21:5* says, *"Careful planning puts you ahead in the long run; hurry and scurry puts you further behind."* (MSG) I think it's safe to say you are tired of hurrying, scurrying, and fumbling around and that you are ready for results. Take the time to make a plan.

Knowing what is most important to you helps create a plan. Having a plan makes the decision-making process much easier. The journey of life is a pathway filled with choices. Some choices are bad, some are good, and some are God. When you know what your priorities are, you can make choices that serve them. If pleasing people is your first priority, when you find yourself faced with making a choice, you make the choice to show up and serve people. The challenge with having pleasing people as your priority is that there are a lot of people in this world. So, depending on how many people you are trying to please at any given moment, pleasing all of them may become problematic and overwhelming. On the other hand, if pleasing God is your first priority, no matter what dilemma you find yourself in and no matter how difficult the choice is, your decision is made easier when you choose to show up and serve God. This doesn't mean you become stiff, religious, or too heavenly-minded too be any earthly good. What it does mean is that when God is your priority, you are privileged and empowered to serve God by showing up and being fully present with His people. And that, my sister, is pure joy. Take the time to prioritize, plan, and show up.

E — Evaluate Emotions

God gave you emotions for a reason. And for that reason, you should honor your emotions. Your emotions were given to you by God to inform and motivate you. Do not resist feeling your emotions. They can help you to survive, thrive, and avoid danger. Your emotions should inform you, not conform you. Be consistent in taking time to evaluate your emotions. Use them to inform you of the alignment or misalignment of your beliefs, attitudes, and actions. Once you are informed, honor your emotions rather than suppress them. You don't want to operate in the false belief that ignoring and burying your emotions makes them disappear. Or that if you ignore them for long enough, they will disappear. Neither of those beliefs deal with the root, they only deal with the fruit. Only when you are willing to sit in your emotions and examine why you are feeling what you are feeling will you be able to move forward in emotional health.

Making time and space for ongoing evaluation ensures that you remain FOCUSed. And when you remain FOCUSed on your emotional health, you can show up and respond to others in a healthy and productive way. And because like spirits attract, you will find that you are attracting people who are aware of and open to evaluating and improving their emotional health.

C — Cooperate

Be aware that R-E-S-I-S-T is always in the midst of irresistible. You can cooperate or compete with the process. Competing with the process is counter-productive, not to mention draining. You don't want to spend your time figuring out how to maneuver around, find a loophole in, or manipulate the steps.

The FOCUS framework is being given to you for your benefit, but if you don't work according to the framework, it will not benefit you. Choose to cooperate with the process rather than resist it. Make up your mind that no matter what, you are going to live in it, work through it, and walk it out. When the process feels good, cooperate with it. When the process doesn't make sense to you, cooperate with it. Doing what has always felt right and made sense to you was not working in the past. It will not produce your desired outcome. However, trusting God with all your heart and not leaning to your own understanding, acknowledging Him in everything you do, and allowing Him to direct your paths will produce an outcome that is better than good.

T — Talk

✓ **T**ell God and your coach: God has already made a way for you to escape every temptation you will ever face. Talk to God and confess your weakness. Remember, in your weakness, His strength is perfected. Share your thoughts, emotions, and desires with your coach. She is there to provide support and guidance.

✓ **A**dmit, apologize and amend: As soon as you realize you have erred, admit your wrongdoing to the one you did the wrong too. Apologize, be honest, and explain your behavior. Make amends by responding with just behavior to restore the relationship. Remember that you are not responsible for, nor can you control, the response of anyone other than yourself. Your responsibility is to humble yourself by admitting your mistake, making the apology, and offering amends.

✓ **L**isten to the wisdom of your coach and accountability partners. They are on the journey with you for support, strength, and wisdom. "*Two are better than one because they have a good return for their labor. For if either of them falls, the one will lift up his companion. But woe to the one who falls when there is not another to lift him up.*" (*Ecclesiastes 4:10,* MSG)

✓ **K**now your limits. Establishing healthy boundaries is a major factor in respecting yourself. Do not think more highly of yourself than you should. Do not set yourself up for failure. This may require that you decline some invitations or separate yourself from some people and places, but you are worth it. *"Do not be deceived, bad company corrupts good morals."* (*1 Corinthians 15:33*, AMP)

Bringing Respect into FOCUS

Respecting yourself is one of the greatest ways you can ensure that you are being respected. It keeps you from falling back into old patterns of thinking and familiar habits.

Do not limit yourself by only doing a check-up from the neck up. Do a complete check-up by tuning in to your body, soul, and spirit. Where are you physically, mentally, emotionally, and spiritually?

1) What BS has tried to reemerge? How have you handled it?

_____

_____

_____

_____

_____

_____

_____

2) How are you embracing the changes you are experiencing?

_____

_____

_____

_____

3) What measures have you taken to make sure you are not moving too fast?

_____

_____

_____

_____

4) Write out and list your priorities. How will this help you in your everyday life?

_____

_____

_____

_____

_____

_____

_____

_____

_____

5) Take time to do an emotional evaluation. Where are you emotionally? How have your values changed since your last evaluation? How is the change impacting your life?

_____

_____

_____

_____

_____

6) In what ways are you cooperating with the FOCUS process? In what ways are you competing? How is your competitiveness sabotaging your progress?

_____

_____

_____

_____

_____

7) God, coach, accountability partners: Who is easiest for you to talk to? Who is it most difficult to talk to? How come?

_____

_____

_____

_____

_____

8) What do you find hardest about acknowledging, admitting, and apologizing? What makes it hard for you?

_____

_____

_____

_____

_____

9) What are some ways you think you can improve your listening skills?

_____

_____

_____

_____

10) Knowing your boundaries requires you know your strengths and weaknesses. What are your strengths and weaknesses?

_____

_____

_____

_____

_____

_____

Use the answers to these questions as points of prayer during your quiet time.

CHAPTER 16

Dealing with the RESIST of Irresistible

There are two real dangers of placing too much emphasis on the destination. One is missing out on the richness of the journey. The other is thinking the goal is to "arrive." Don't get it twisted. The richness of the journey is not found in the success of reaching the destination; rather, it is experienced in the significance of living in your destiny.

Blurry Vision

Trisha could not figure out why the approach of Valentine's Day was causing her to feel so anxious. She had come so far in her healing process. But in the past few weeks, she had spent a lot of time on the Internet trolling for prospective dates. She could tell things were about to get out of control. She had spent the last hour sitting in her car in front of the gym. She'd parked the car with the intention of going inside to work out for an hour. Before she got out of the car, she'd checked her phone for any pings or prospects. Her quick check had turned into an hour. Trish realized she was operating in what she affectionately called OTB, short for "old Trisha behavior."

She was enjoying her new life, at least up until a couple of weeks ago. She wasn't sure what happened to cause her to start stepping backwards. A conversation with one her accountability partners was long overdue. The phone was already in her hand, so she stopped resisting, and made the call.

> *"I'm not saying that I have this all together, that I have it made. But I am well on my way, reaching out for Christ, who has so wondrously reached out for me. Friends, don't get me wrong: By no means do I count myself an expert in all of this, but I've got my eye on the goal, where God is beckoning us onward — to Jesus. I'm off and running, and I'm not turning back."*
>
> *Philippians 3: 12-14 (MSG)*

A Lifestyle, Not an Event

When you follow the FOCUS Framework, you will undoubtedly experience transformation. As your beliefs, desires, and behaviors begin coming into FOCUS, you will be able to see more clearly, follow more nearly, and love more dearly, day by day. You will begin to notice how the changes inside of you are positively impacting what is going on around you. You will notice that you are beginning to attract a different caliber of people, people who are traveling the same road you are traveling. You are having a new experience in life, not because things are changing, but because you are changing. You are beginning to see how all things are working for your good. Good things are happening for you and to you. You are free to make choices based on your priorities. You realize that instead of freaking out when storms arise, you have peace. You realize that instead of avoiding challenges, you now see challenges as an opportunity for growth. You find that at times the joy you are experiencing is causing you to smile unexplainably, laugh uncontrollably, and love unrestrained. This is what life irresistible is all about, and you, my sister, are beginning to live it.

In the midst of your living, I don't want you to get distracted. Remember, R-E-S-I-S-T is always hanging out in the midst of irresistibility. It is easy to slip and fall back into old habits. If you don't believe me, ask someone who has developed healthy habits. It is important that you resist the thoughts and behaviors that will sabotage your desires. The acronym RESIST will shed some light on the obstacles you will face, so you can be prepared and avoid slipping back into your old ways.

RESIST

R — Realize

Realize you will be tested. Yes, people from your past will show up and get on your last nerve — I'm talking about your *reserved* nerve. Every day will come with its own opportunities, circumstances, and situations. Realizing that challenges will present themselves is the first step of resisting doubt and fear. It gives you the heads-up so you can be prepared. There is no need for you to pretend you have it all together. You have tools. Use them.

Realize your greatest defense and offense are found in your relationships with God, yourself, your coach, and your accountability partners. God is able to handle anything and everything that shows up in you and in your life. In fact, God is faithful not to give you more than you can handle and to make a way of escape from temptation (*1 Corinthians 10:13*). You are equipped, empowered, and victorious. You are not alone. You have people who have already seen you with your makeup and your mask off, and who accept and love you for who you are. So, resist the thoughts of rejection, worthlessness, and isolation.

Realize that you cannot control every event of your life. You can, however, decide how you will respond to them. Challenges will arise. Take responsibility for your respond-ability. Remember that forgiveness is one of the most powerful weapons in your bag of stones. Also remember that forgiveness is a process. Stick with the process, so you can enjoy the freedom of not being bound to an offense and or an offender. You will fall short of God's glory. Forgive yourself and receive God's forgiveness. You have the power to receive and give forgiveness. Resist thoughts of powerlessness.

Realize your ability to take on responsibility is greatly connected to your ability to respond. Through Christ, you have the gained the power to respond instead of react. You no longer have to hand your power over to someone or something else. Procrastination, fear, and excuses no longer control you. It's not because you know every answer or every outcome. It's because you are in an intimate relationship with the One who holds every answer and controls every outcome. Trust that everything is going to work for your good (*Proverbs 3:4-10* AMP).

E — Every Day, One Day at a Time

Make sure that you don't get so caught up in enjoying your life that you forget to move forward one day at a time. Living in the past and living in the future both rob you of the gift of living in the present. Use each day as an opportunity for growth by looking at your actions — both the good and the bad. Consider how you could have responded differently and celebrate the good decisions you made. Be aware of how doubt, fear, and resentment impacted your day and celebrate how you honored your priorities. Resist operating in denial, deception, and co-dependency.

S — Stay Accountable

Keeping it real requires that you stay accountable to God, yourself, and others. Your coach and accountability partners are not there just for the journey. The relationships you have with them are likely the purest, most unpretentious relationships you will ever have. Stay connected. Life happens, and the possibility of distance, distraction, and a host of other things will present. Talking with your coach and accountability partners will keep you from becoming stagnant or reverting.

Remember that you will have to be deliberate about staying connected. Plan an annual gathering to celebrate life! Stay accountable by remaining answerable to your thoughts, words, and actions. Be on the lookout for BS: blame, shame, bitterness, selfishness, boasting, and self-pity. It will try to slide back into your life. But you can resist BS by using your tools. And when you resist it, it will have to flee. Use your tool of accountability to help you identify the reappearance of any old patterns and behaviors.

I — Implementation

It is not enough for you to know what you ought to do. Information without application and implementation does not yield transformation. You will need to stay committed to do what you know. You will not profit in transition if you choose to hear without acting. Implementing what you have learned has proven critical to the transformation you have experienced so far, and its importance doesn't diminish. Continue to walk the talk.

Doing daily, monthly, and annual inventories will help you be aware of and stay on top of your progress. Evaluate and ask yourself if your values and actions are in alignment. If your will is completely surrendered to God. If you have you totally received the forgiveness of God. Be intentional. Don't believe the hype that you don't have time for evaluating where you are physically, psychologically, emotionally, and spiritually. You are worth more than the time you schedule. When the voice inside your head tells you that you are too busy to stop, drop (to your knees), and slow your roll. Take it as a sign that stop, drop, and slow your roll is exactly what you need to do. Stop drop, and roll is a fire safety prevention program. Ignoring the process can result in burns, pain, and fatality. Honoring the process can save your life.

S — Sincerity

Your past wants to hold onto you even though you are moving forward. You will most likely experience the emergence of feelings and emotions from time to time. Do not run from your emotions. Do not try to avoid or suppress your feelings. Be sincere in that your responses are free from pretense and deceit. Don't attempt to manipulate or control a situation or another person. Depend on God to help you respond and proceed from the resources of His genuine feelings.

Letting go of the insult and the injury through forgiveness may be one of the greatest challenges of moving forward. Your ability to release and receive is going to determine your ability to resist slipping back into negative thoughts, feelings, and behaviors. Your ability to extend forgiveness is directly dependent on your ability to receive forgiveness. If you feel that somehow you're paying for your wrong, or that you have to earn forgiveness from God, you will make others pay and earn your forgiveness. The forgiveness given to you is a gift of God's grace. There was and is nothing you can do to earn it.

Offering forgiveness is in no way a weakness on your part. Forgiving does not mean you are denying that you have been wronged. It means that even though you have been wronged, you make the choice to release yourself from the bondage and power of the offense and the offender. You are responding to the grace and forgiveness you received from God through Jesus Christ. You are giving for the sake of your freedom. The power to forgive comes from God. Receive God's forgiveness, release the wrongdoers, and rejoice in the freedom of forgiveness.

When you make the decision to forgive, you may not experience an immediate feeling of release. What I'm saying is that when you offer forgiveness, the act of forgiveness is complete, but it may take your feelings a while to catch up with it. If you operate according to your feelings, you will think that you didn't really forgive. Remember, forgiveness does not always happen instantaneously. It's a process that becomes more doable as you do it.

Be sincere in expressing your feelings and in forgiving and resisting the bondage that comes with unforgiveness. You can forgive and still be hurt. The difference is that you allow the hurt to heal rather than paralyze you. Be sincere when you make amends.

T — Trust

You are not, in your own power, strong enough to gain or maintain life irresistible. It is only through the power of God the Father, Son, and Holy Spirit that you will have such an experience. You are God's beloved and He cares for you. Put your trust in Him. Trust that He will be your strength when you are weak. Trust that He is the source of all that you need. Trust that He will never leave you alone or forsake you. Trust that God is able. There will be times when you will question why things are happening like they are happening. How come you are being treated like you are being treated? How come you didn't get the job or the promotion? How come someone didn't invite you to the event? When those questions arise, approach them with trust; trust that there is purpose in it and that it will work out for your good in the end. Rely on, depend on, and fully rest in God, His will, His way, and His timing. Placing your trust in God, as opposed to people, places, and things, will give you the strength you need to resist doubt and discouragement.

Irresistibility is not for the faint of heart. It requires patience, strength, and tenacity. The tools that helped you confront, commence, and conquer are the same tools that will help you maintain your FOCUS. There will be times when you will have to go back and work a key. In fact, the FOCUS Framework is not intended to be an event. It is intended to be a lifestyle framework. The more you FOCUS, the more you learn about God, yourself, and others, and the more you experience an irresistible life. I want you to remember the words that are written on this page. You have already shown the strength of your commitment and tenacity by moving through the FOCUS Framework. You are loved. You are valuable. And you are able.

The RESIST Factor

Dealing with the R-E-S-I-S-T factor is a necessity for life irresistible. I do not want to mislead you or cause you to believe keeping your life in FOCUS is easy or that there is a shortcut. The truth is that there will be times when you feel hard pressed on every side or abandoned. There will be times when you feel like your meekness is being mistaken for weakness and that you are being taken advantage of. You will cry until you feel like you don't have any more tears to shed. And just when you think it is all coming together and it is all good, you will experience feelings of insecurity, vulnerability, and overwhelm. It doesn't mean you are weak, it means you are human. Acknowledging feelings of resistance does not mean that something is wrong with you; it means that you are aware of your internal battle. Use the tools listed above to deal with the resistance.

You are beginning to experience life irresistible. You are operating in the power of clarity as you gain understanding of who and Whose you are. You have gained wisdom, knowledge, and tools to help you FOCUS. You are enjoying freedom and peace like never before. When you look back over your life, the life you are living now seems a bit surreal. Be assured, the life you are living is real and the best is yet to come. Ensuring that your experience will continue is the result of strategic planning. You can win the battle, but you will always be at war. Strategy is a necessity.

1) Realizing your responsibility and respond-ability are based
    in your relationship with God. How will you maintain
    and nurture your relationship with God?

    _____

    _____

    _____

    _____

2) How will evaluating your thoughts, beliefs, and behaviors
    benefit you? What is your evaluation strategy?

    _____

    _____

    _____

    _____

3) What action will you take to ensure you remain accountable
    for your actions?

    _____

    _____

    _____

    _____

4) What is the connection between receiving forgiveness from God and extending pardon to others? What is your strategy for forgiveness?

_____

_____

_____

_____

5) How has receiving God's forgiveness set you free? How will forgiving others impact you?

_____

_____

_____

_____

CHAPTER 17

Conclusion

You can spend your time running from your past or running towards your future. In both scenarios, you are running, but in the latter, you are looking forward, more aware of where you are, and excited about where you are going.

The FOCUS Framework

The culet of a diamond is the tiny point at the base of the diamond. The more focused and precise the cut of the diamond, the better the light reflects through the stone. The more light that reflects through the stone, the more fire and brilliance the stone displays. Making practical and effective use of the FOCUS Framework will allow the light of God's love to operate in and through you, making the passion and brilliance in you reflective. This reflective quality of God's love is what irresistible life is all about.

Incorporating the FOCUS Framework into your lifestyle enables you to move forward with the emphasis on knowing who you are, whose you are, and how valuable you are. By evaluating your past, you will be able to value the gift of living in the now, and have hope for the future. Let's do a quick review of the Focus Framework

F — Figure It Out

Figure out what you believe, what you desire, and what is blocking you. You can have more than one hundred thoughts within an hour. Your beliefs are the thoughts to which you give power. Figuring out your beliefs provides you with the power of knowledge. Know what you believe and you know the foundation of your attitude and behavior.

Your desires are powerful in determining the probability of fulfilling your destiny. When you invite Him to place His desires in your heart, you position yourself to experience more than you could ever ask for, think, or imagine. You also posture yourself for victory, because if God wants it. God will ensure that it comes to past. So, ask God to give you the desires of your heart (*Psalm 37:4*).

When you encounter an obstacle that seems insurmountable, take a moment to see which direction you are facing. Most insurmountable obstacles are in your past, but they are casting a shadow and impacting how you are experiencing your current reality and how you are viewing the future. Remember two things about shadows. First, shadows have the ability to appear larger than the actual object. Second, shadows are cast when an object is blocking light. Remove the object, and the shadow goes away. If the shadow is being cast from your presence, check your positioning. When the Son, I mean sun, is high and lifted up, all shadows are underfoot.

O — Observe, Operate in Openness and Obey

Observe what you are thinking, feeling, and believing, and you will understand why you are behaving as you do. Observe your behavior, and you will gain insight on what you think, feel, and believe. Observe with openness so you can live in the open, with a soul and spirit that relies on God and His power. Remember, one of the hardest things to open is a closed mind. Be open to doing it differently, whatever it may be — think differently, talk differently, develop a different attitude and approach. Don't try to avoid the four-letter word "obey." When you obey, your life will become less overwhelming and more manageable.

C — Confront, Commence, and Conquer

Your ability to confront your past rests in your ability to put your confidence in God, operate in faith, and nip fear in the bud. When you do this, you get in front of overpowering feelings and regret. By keeping your mind occupied with the things of God, nourishing the truth, and trusting in God, you are equipped with everything you need and can get in front of the con (whatever it is that is standing against you).

Commencing is the beginning of retrieving your God-given power and authority. Sometimes it is necessary to retreat before you advance. The purpose of retreating is to step back, regroup, and strategize internally. By taking time to identify individuals, note the incidents, state the impact, investigate the injury, determine the impact, and eliminate the erroneous, you are actually suiting up and preparing to strategically dismantle your obstacles.

Conquering is your act of committing, openly examining, naming emotions, questioning impacts, exchanging the negative for the positive, and remembering whose side you are on. If God is for you, who can be successful in their attack against you? You are more than a conqueror through Christ Jesus!

U — Understand and Use What You Have

Abuse and neglect are often the result of misunderstanding. After all, it is difficult to properly utilize something when you don't understand what it is and how it operates. Understanding the gift of God's grace enables you to operate in the guaranteed victory, redemptive power, acceptance, comfort, and encouragement of all God has done for you! Victory is yours. So, use what you have. You may feel broken-hearted, but you are not empty-handed. Use what's in your hand, or, should I say, keep your hand in the hand of Jesus. Your growing relationship with Him will help you gain confidence, remember the redemptive work of the Cross, approach all things with humility and forgiveness, communicate with the Comforter, and be encouraged. You've got this, because Jesus has you.

S — Stand firm and Stay FOCUSed

Too many people find that their intelligence can get them into places where their character can't keep them. Well, none of that is happening here. Living a lifestyle of FOCUS ensures that you share your challenges and victories, take and make time to concentrate, bring your "A" Game — admit, apologize, make amends, note your progress, and do a FOCUS test. You do not have to fall prey to your history or mystery. You have what you need to stand firm and stay focused.

Staying focused is a result of respecting yourself. Don't expend your energy on trying to make someone respect you. Take time to recognize your old behaviors, embrace change, slow your roll, prioritize, evaluate your emotions, cooperate with the process, and TALK. You will have respect — the respect of God and of yourself.

FOCUS Your Energy; Experience True Love

Writing this book is one of the most challenging endeavors that I have voluntarily agreed to do. The challenge was not in creating the content. I know about resisting the irresistible, because I did it for years. I know the heaviness, darkness, and emptiness of living with unhealed hurts, unmet needs, and unresolved issues, and I know the joy, beauty, and freedom of living in light and lightness of irresistible life. I know how FOCUSing helped me to move out of the darkness into the light. I have the blessing of peace instead of depression and loneliness when I put my head on my pillow at night. I experience the joy and freedom of waking up to the new mercies of God and live my day under His umbrella of His grace. I live in the confidence that I am tremendously loved by God. The challenge was making the time to keep the commitment. Life kept happening — in fact, it seemed to accelerate and intensify. When I felt overwhelmed and couldn't make time or focus my thoughts, I thought of you. You are the catalyst that fueled my passion.

Knowing that you are feeling lonely instead of loved and that you are experiencing tainted love rather than true love kept me up and typing during the night. Knowing that your past is negatively impacting your current reality and attempting to cancel your future is what caused me to wake up and start typing before the sun rose. It is because I know that healing, deliverance, and the freedom to live an irresistible life are experiences you deserve that I carried my laptop with me when I took my vacation. I could not — I will not sit quietly while my sisters are hurting.

Prayers are ascending that the Holy Spirit uses the words recorded on these pages to transform your life, and that your desire and willingness to FOCUS provides healing for the wounds of your heart, reconciliation for brokenness of your soul, and revival for the downturn of your spirit.

Please know how much you are loved, how valuable you are, and how strong you are. You are fearfully and wonderfully made. You are a work of art crafted by the same hands that crafted the universe. You are an original, uniquely designed by God; there is no one else like you.

My hope is that you will focus not on your past, but on the framework provided within these pages, and that you will apply what you read and experience transformation. I hope that you do not resist what God has prepared for you, and that you make the choice to receive God's unfailing love, walk in His amazing grace, accept His unmatched forgiveness, experience His unspeakable joy, and live filled within His irresistible goodness.

Now What?

Now that you know my desire for you, have read the book, begun the process, and are starting to experience transformation, your next step is to ensure that you do all you can do to keep your life in FOCUS. You don't want to slip and fall off the edge. As much as I would love to, I can't guarantee that you won't slip back into your old habits or fall prey to a crapload of emotional BS.

But what I can do is to assure you that you can FOCUS and begin living an irresistible life. I can also avail myself to walk the journey with you, serving as your coach. As your coach my commitment would be to show you the way and hold you accountable. Simply go to www.makemeirresistible.com and schedule your complementary Four Cs assessment today.

Here are testimonies from two of the many women I have coached. I look forward to reading the testimony you write based on your irresistible journey very soon.

From Losing to Love — *Lynn's Testimony*
Coach Trina,

Thank you seems so inadequate as an express of the gratitude that I have in my heart for you. The uniqueness of your gifting is that you don't use your own words; meaning that everything you say is rooted in scripture. You apply ancient writings into today's complex chaotic world.

You emphasized God's words to gently guide me into living life more abundantly. When first approached with the concept of having a life coach, I was naturally resistant. To share my life completely and honestly with another human was so far beyond my comprehension. However, I had been on anti-depressants at the request of my former supervisor, my life was out of my control and my emotions were unmanageable. I was a train wreck about to happen, so I didn't have much to lose.

The first relationship that we dealt with was my relationship with myself. Coach Trina taught me how to take to broken pieces of my life and turn them into peace. An inner peace that is beyond understanding. Getting FOCUSed is more than an acronym, it is a lifestyle change. To truly experience Irresistible love, I had to first learn to love the person that God created me to be. For me that meant discovering the person within, the one that had been suppressed for years or even decades. Then finding the love of God that has been waiting for me to receive it as freely as it has been given.

It is amazing to me that I am free enough now to even use the word love. I had banned the word from my working vocabulary due to the hurt, pain and disappointments that I had experienced in the name of love. To me love was just another profane four-letter word. That is what Coach Trina does. She enables you to experience the love and light that is in Christ, all while not promoting religion. She merely directs you on the path to wholeness and emotional stability through the manifestation of acknowledging God's love in your life. Being FOCUSed changed the entire paradigm of my existence. Where I was once bitter, angry, full of darkness and rage, I now have peace of mind and spirit, the love of God and the light which is in Christ. "Thank you, Coach Trina", seems so inadequate to express my gratitude for making me irresistible.

Love you,

Lynn Roberson

Don't Know How, But He Did It — Teresa's Testimony

Before coaching I was stuck on rewind. After 28 years the divorce was final, and I could not see how to move a single step forward from that point. My life as I knew it was ended and I had no drive or knowledge of how to go forward from there. I was a bucket of pain, regret and spiritual starvation. Hurt that the continuation of hope for married for life, becoming grandma and grandpa together, had come to an end. I felt it was entirely my fault because I could not change myself to fit or please another person. I felt unliked and unlikeable; unloved and unlovable. I was fearful. I had no career and overnight I went from middle class to poverty just like that. I was too broken to even fight for my future in the divorce settlement. I wanted my children to be alright even though I was far from it. I prayed but never thought to listen for God's voice, certain that the Almighty would not talk to me. But He did. He sent Trina Petersen. She looked like warm sunshine in the midst of the terrible storm I was living in. She acted like she didn't see the mean storm surrounding me. She offered kindness, and peace, and gentle encouragement. She seemed to be able to see me through the horrible creature I had become. She seemed to hold out her hand and say to me, 'Sister, God sent me for you. Let's go.' I cannot bear to think where I would be if she had not come.

During coaching I experienced a difficult five years! I almost died so many times. I would rewind and relive the marriage and almost die. I would rewind and relive the separation and almost die. I would rewind and relive the divorce and try very hard to die. For better or for worse I wanted him back. I wanted my life with him back, even if it killed me. I did not know how to live without trying to please him. Long ago I had stopped living for God and had been living for the look of a happy marriage. When the marriage failed, I failed. How does one so foolish and misguided gain insight and understanding? I don't know exactly how, but God used Coach Trina.

My irresistible journey has been a long journey. Transformation takes time and you better have some help. Coach Trina helped me. She has understanding because she has been through some things. She has knowledge that comes from experience and insight because of her relationship with God. She has wisdom.

Since embarking on my irresistible journey, I have learned to stop trying to go back to situations I have been delivered from and to be grateful for deliverance. I have learned to stop going against God by walking into tempting situations, and instead to trust Him in everything and allowing Him to direct my paths. I have found comfort, confidence and stability in God. Joshua 1:9 says, "Have I not commanded you? Be strong and courageous. Do not be afraid; do not be discouraged, for the Lord your God will be with you wherever you go." And I have learned to love myself; the woman God created and Jesus died for; a person so special that the hairs on my head are numbered. My life has begun anew.

This is transformation — "a thorough or dramatic change in form or appearance." For me, transformation happened because Coach Trina answered the call on her life to help others. Without her, I would have limped on through life not knowing or experiencing the goodness and love God has for me. Thank you, Coach Trina.

Teresa

Resources

Scripture quotations identified AMP are taken from the Amplified® Bible (AMP), copyright © 2015 by The Lockman Foundation. Used by permission. www.Lockman.org.

Scripture quotations identified NIV are taken from THE HOLY BIBLE, NEW INTERNATIONAL VERSION®, NIV® Copyright © 1973, 1978, 1984, 2011 by Biblica, Inc.® Used by permission. All rights reserved worldwide.

Scripture quotations marked MSG are taken from *The Message*. Copyright © 1993, 1994, 1995, 1996, 2000, 2001, 2002. Used by permission of NavPress Publishing Group.

Acknowledgements

Writing this book was a labor of love that began late in the evening on February 26, 2017. That is when I decided, based on a feeling in my "knower," to respond to a Facebook ad for writers who want to make a difference. My action was spontaneous, taken with little thought and fueled by my passion. I have a passion for facilitating healing among women. I also know that the mess of my history is my ministry for this present age. So, I said a prayer, brought my mess and this age together, and allowed God to pen this message through my head, heart, and hand. I received this as a great opportunity to help someone else. I never imagined I would gain so much from the experience. Thank you, Angela Lauria of The Author Incubator, for posting your ad, believing in me, and requiring me to show up.

Next, I want to give a big shout-out of thanks to my family, especially my daughters, sister, and mother, for loving me through this journey. Many years ago, it became evident to me that I was a hurt person who was hurting people, people that I loved. It is your unconditional love that encouraged me to change. It is a result of your unconditional love and encouragement that I found the courage to write. Words cannot express how thankful I am for your continued patience and graciousness even as I was writing this book. You listened without complaint as I went through the process of getting the words from my head, through my heart, and onto the paper.

I am equally thankful for the women who hold me accountable. Sharing the journey, shedding tears, sharing laughter, and celebrating the victories have developed a sister bond that holds a special place in my heart. Your words of encouragement, hugs, prayers, and presence continue to give me strength.

To those who have allowed me the privilege and the honor to share in their journey. You will never know how humbled I am to have been chosen, by you, to walk this journey of transformation with you. You trusted me and allowed me to enter places that remain secret to many. I do not take that lightly. Nor do I take for granted your generosity in allowing me to share your stories. Your willingness to be transparent speaks to your growth, courage, and compassion.

To the Morgan James Publishing team: Special thanks to David Hancock, CEO & Founder for believing in me and my message. To my Author Relations Manager, Gayle West, thanks for making the process seamless and easy. Many more thanks to everyone else, but especially Jim Howard, Bethany Marshall, and Nickcole Watkins.

Last, but certainly not least, I thank my Heavenly Father for preventing the weapons that were formed against me from prospering, for creating a way of escape, and for working everything together for the good! Your gift of Jesus and the Holy Spirit gave me everything I needed to share my tests as testimonies and turn my mess into my message. Great are Your mercy and grace towards me! I am forever grateful.

About the Author

Trina Petersen is a life coach and a pastor. She is an author, successful entrepreneur, and keynote speaker. She specializes in helping women break free from emotional and spiritual bondage and gain the freedom to love, live, and pursue their dreams. She has spent the last 13 years working with women one-on-one and in group settings. Firsthand experience equips her with wisdom, tenacity, and compassion. Trina is passionate about helping women a) identify their passion and b) use it as the framework for maximizing their potential and enjoying life. Her "keeping it real" approach equips, empowers, and encourages women to emerge from the shadows of life to live lives of significance. It's who she is and what she does.

Trina has been privileged to be shaped by and work with distinguished professionals, including Dr. John Patton and Dr. Carolyn

McCrary. She holds a Bachelor of Science in Biblical Education from Beulah Heights University, a Masters of Divinity from The Interdenominational Theological Center, has completed 8 units of CPE (Clinical Pastoral Education), and is a member of the John Maxwell Team. Trina combines her education, entrepreneurial spirit, and her experience as a time management organizational systems consultant to provide dynamic transformative coaching experiences. The phenomenal transformation of those she has worked with fuels her passion. Trina is excited to expand into the public population with her personalized life coaching program, seminars, retreats, books, and speaking engagements.

Trina currently resides outside of Atlanta, GA. She loves spending time with her family, especially her grandson. Trina also enjoys crafting, experiencing new cultures, and meeting new people.

Website: www.makemeirresistible.com

Email: CoachTrina@makemeirresistible.com

Facebook: TrinaPetersen

Thank You

We have covered a lot of territory in this book. If you have truly FOCUSed on the lessons and worked the keys, you are beginning to experience the irresistible life you desire. You understand that irresistible life does not exclude you from encountering resistance, the R-E-S-I-S-T is always present, but God's grace provides you with what you need, not only to survive, but to overcome, transform, and thrive. As life would have it, change doesn't happen at a convenient time, nor does it come with an easy button. Rather, transformation is in process.

I want to be transparent with you. Sharing the events in this book is part of my FOCUS process. I share with you in hopes of encouraging you. I care about you and hope that my words have a positive impact on your life. I would love for you to share your FOCUS experience with me and with other women who are praying for a way of escape from the internal wilderness they are existing in and for the strength to FOCUS. Go to www.makemeirresistible.com and click on the "Sharing Is Caring" button to share your experience.

You can also go to www.makemeirresistible.com and click on the "FOCUS Tools" button. There you will find a copy of the inventory sheet for INSIDE and a copy of the INSIDE Inventory Sheet as promised. You will also, find a few other helpful surprises.

Stop allowing unhealed hurts, unmet needs, and unresolved issues to dominate your life and cause you to resist irresistible life. Make yourself a priority. Get your notebook and pen, go to the website, download your tools, put on something comfortable, and begin to FOCUS.

Morgan James
Speakers Group

www.TheMorganJamesSpeakersGroup.com

We connect Morgan James published authors with live and online events and audiences who will benefit from their expertise.

Morgan James makes all of our titles available
through the Library for All Charity Organization.

www.LibraryForAll.org

Printed in the USA
CPSIA information can be obtained
at www.ICGtesting.com
JSHW082205140824
68134JS00014B/437

9 781683 508137